UNEVEN LANES

POETRY BY
John V. Jones Jr.

on all the highways
you choose to travel
you will encounter
uneven lanes

Austin, August 2015

Contents

Answering the Call

Reflections on Cyclical Journeys

Something About Midnight: Prose Poems

Author's Note

I remember in college a literature prof telling me that if one desired to be a poet, then such a path precluded the possibility of financial stability. One could be a poet only if one were set to be hungry, destitute, and at least six months behind rent. So it seemed. For this reason, I do not take on the epithet of poet. I'm basically an amateur writer of various types of genre including short stories, articles, and blogs. I wrote these poems over a period of several years. (Each poem in the collection is dated at the time of its completion.) Moreover, I wrote them for the simple fun of it. They entail various themes, settings, protagonists, and emotions. I don't consider myself a serious poet, but I hope if someone falls across this self-published collection, he or she can garner some enjoyment from the encounter.

I suppose a word about the various themes is in order. Readers will note some Christian themes in several of the poems. I am a Christian, and Judeo-Christianity forms my worldview although I did not set out to write what can be called *Christian poetry*. The themes about which I write vary. In as much as I want my writing to be about living life, I will touch on anything where it seems appropriate – upbeat, dark, foreboding, mysterious, searching, concrete, uplifting, and spiritual. All these themes or subjects are worth writing about because they cover the full gamut of human experience. We are all on our personal paths, whether or not we realize it. At times we vary from that path, both in known and unknown ways. There are times that we go places we shouldn't go. Then we find ourselves searching to get back on track.

I suppose I should also offer a word regarding Haiku poetry. The section in which my forty or so Haiku poems are presented is called, *Playing with Haiku*. And that's exactly what I'm doing. I don't consider myself an expert on Haiku poetry on any level, other than I've always enjoyed reading it. I decided to try my hand at it. Haiku poetry owns a long and honorable position in poetics. The poems in this form speak to a philosophical take on life, usually from the perspective of Zen and other Oriental ways of thinking and engaging life. This poetic form concretizes experience, generally describing something in nature, or some concrete experience encountered in life, and then takes the reader to a transcendent view that doesn't negate the concrete experience, but places it in the stream and cycles of life. A couple of things are important here that I want to clarify. First, I'm *having fun with*, not *making fun of* Haiku. I recognize and appreciate its venerable history in poetics. Second, I do not approach the level of the great poets in this ancient poetic form, nor was I seeking to do so. As one will gather from the various Haiku verse in this collection, I wanted to have some fun exploring different themes via the Haiku form. Western and Christian rather than Eastern philosophy, personal memory, etc. make the line-up for the Haiku verse I've written. I write out some of the Haiku poems based on Old and New Testament themes, utilizing the form in the sense of a prayer. Some of the Haiku poems I included here touch on the themes of the longer poems in the collection. Readers will come across such themes as Vampires, werewolves, natural wolves, etc., all written simply to have some fun. I do not think that any of these treatments violate or disparage the Haiku tradition. All the poems are written in a 5-7-5 structure. Haiku is a poetic form that I enjoy reading, as well as taking it on in a playful, lighthearted, but respectful manner.

All in all, what is presented here is a collection of poems that I played around with in terms of style, theme, and structure, all written for the sake of having fun. I claim nothing else. I do hope those who might peradventure encounter these pages find some enjoyment.

John V. Jones, Jr.
Austin, TX
February 6, 2019

UNEVEN
LANES

DRIVING INTO MIDNIGHT

A Misanthrope's Meditation

I now possess
my sought out desert
forever basking in
sun burnt anger, arid madness
and rippling heat waves of hate
where desertion is not a curse.
Sandblasted face
dryness
in dry heat
cactus filled life
Gila monster's poison
sidewinder's strike
scorpion's curled tail,
all emerge from
a parched tongue
baked skin and
stroked-ripped mind.
Blurred burnt vision thrives
where there is no thought,
passions cracked like
desiccated ponds
enclosed within a floor of
scorched sand surrounded by
paradoxes where haunting beauty lies,
where deadly heat and flaming siroccos
fold into chilled night winds.
Here lies despised territory

for which I longed
walking dryly in a direction
where there is no journey,
traveling a straight line
round and round
entrenched in and castigated for
my *truths*,
demented by
misinterpreted stoicism.
I have taken my stand
not seeking forgiveness
in the eye of
a whirlwind of grit
where sand storms
blow the sun
to distant places
where cool rains taunt
with portraits of life
I thought I understood,
willfully shirked,
knowingly discarded,
but in truth
never knew.

Austin, June 2013

A Sartrean Discourse

Being-in-itself
I am not
Being-for-itself
I step out.

The snarling roots of the tree frighten where
in gray stark coldness all that is real
tells a tale to the soul
about a useless passion.

Hell is other people.
Hell is other people.

Authenticity unfolds on a wave of angst,
bad faith sirens,
expediency beckons
over an abyss of Nonbeing.
Courage annihilates the dark
only to leave the dark
where there is no essence
but that generated by existence.
The mist hangs in the trees,
the nausea gnaws from within
where there is no exit from the war
no escape from decision.
Excuses float and sink
on an abysmal sea

of condemnation
to be free.
Dialectics are realized
in Parisian cafes
over morning cups of *le café*
and grids of typeset in the evening.

If only I had done . . .
you did what you chose.
If I had turned this way . . .
you went the way you turned.
If only I had seen . . .
you see what you saw.
If only I had known . . .
you know what you know and are known.
If I had decided thus . . .
you decided.
If only I had been . . .
you are your choosing.

Being-in-itself
I am only a rock
Being-for-itself
I am a negation in my becoming.

Hell is other people.
Hell is other people.

I am what I choose and what I choose not.

Austin, December 2012

9

Steel on Steel

While my poor bones jostle and roll,
up dances my soul . . .
        —Jules Laforgue

Oh Charlie stole the handle
and the train it won't stop going
no way to slow down.
        —Jethro Tull

Steel on steel
in dreamlike haze
clear glass window
takes in the days
of living, winning, losing.

Metal wheels thunder and quake
lonely whistles break the night
along the line between sleep and wake,
I see the darkness and the light
of living, winning, losing.

Familiar crossroads
rapidly stream by
in the bat of an eye
a thought, a dream, a sigh
belonging to yesterday
long last forgotten;
now emerging from
corridors of time
scenes begin to play

with a recollecting mind
serving pleasure and pain.

Laughing at the fool
in the mirror of time
crying over thoughts
smiling or resigned
hoping to regain
what never returns
rewriting histories
as lessons one learns.

Beautiful eyes fall
on my window
a street name I recall
a face I remember
all held a future
where youthful passions
cut, tore, and sutured;
what if's scream
while steel on steel
roars through the steam.

In dreamlike haze
clear glass window
takes in the days.

A young man watches
the engine pass in the night

a lone figure standing
beneath a streetlight
only a shadow
on outpouring steam
he who had hopes and
a courageous dream
took his fight to the crux
where wins and losses
totaled to a question – *what's next.*

Imprison the wind
close open eyes
would you do it all again
what can't be revised;
read the pages
unfolding in stages
without shame or disguise;
a story some of which I like
some of which I despise.

Figurines stream by
like time unsecured
stinging deep memory
with actions demurred;
impassioned offenses
intimate faces
smiles and frowns
handshakes and embraces
lost in the screeching grind

of steel on steel
and all one can find –

Lonely whistles that break the night
along the line between sleep and wake
I see the darkness and the light.

Philosophies of life
unfurled along the way
consistency lost in strife
putting things off
till another day;
cannot read the end
or start over again,
positions held then released
stands taken and deceased
strewn to the wind
of clanging change.

Wanting to know it all
before my time
trying to live as if
mistakes were a crime,
those charms of wisdom
that I cast from my song
by not confessing
I could be wrong.
A thought, a tear
a gentle laugh

at prizes and fear
and risks that are cached
in stands of valor
in retreats in pain
all flowing in review
in the night's refrain;
with the heat and sweat of
steam upon my brow
the thunder of time's engine
continues to
surrealistically howl,
hammering out steel on steel
bringing me back to now.

In dreamlike haze
clear glass window
takes in the days.

Timelines marked
strength and victory,
dotted with weakness
regret and loss,
longing to be relived
reclaimed and then won
from some Archimedean point
after all has been done;
but time is not altered
nor all that time brings,
the train won't go back

winters follow springs;
it won't stop going,
no reverse gear
the brakeman's gone
destiny feels near.

Lovers come, then they leave
friendships done, then undone
passions are heaved
one-by-one
across the tracks of time;
no rest stations, overnight spots
only places and faces
where the engine never stops,
and memories jump
feeling but a bump,
one time terminal to another.

My summation flows
from an overworked brain,
a story I can tell
and retell but never tame;
the facts are the facts
placed in truth or a lie,
they are who I am;
the only one deceived is I.

And steel on steel keeps rolling
somewhere.

Metal wheels thunder and quake,
lonely whistles break the night
along the line between sleep and wake,
I see the darkness and the light.

In dreamlike haze
clear glass window
takes in the days.

Austin, August, 2013

Journey

Exiting his dream
by choice he departed

      upon a highway
      of dreams that

            pulled him involuntarily
            toward that which he dreamed.

Austin, June 2015

The Confession

Behind the veil of sleep
I stood atop a bare tree
a simulacrum in shape
to the Tree of Life
in a land deep in autumn.

In the storm-filled distance
a funnel cloud raged,
the wind shook the tree,
the limb on which I stood broke.
I struck the ground.

Upon rising and inwardly bruised
I noticed an old Chinese man sitting
behind me in a deep, meditative
trance with a stone, stoic face,
still and silent in a lotus position.

As if the funnel cloud like time had
swept me to that one moment
I looked into his eyes, came to know
what I knew but did not want to know,
spoke the words I did not want to say –

I have done much wrong in my life

Austin, March 2013

Medicinal

I drove down to the river
down to the river
just to watch the water roll.
That water has a way of soothing
deep down in your soul.

That river kept on flowing
kept on flowing
flowing right along.

I journeyed out to the desert
out to the desert
to watch the wind blow across the sand.
That sirocco has a way of speaking
so you know where you stand.

That wind kept on blowing
kept on blowing
blowing right along.

I climbed to the peak of the mountain
the peak of the mountain
to get a closer view of God and the sun.
That mountain has a way of teaching –
Eternity *is* the long run.

The world kept on turning
kept on turning
turning right along.

Austin, October 2013

Inner Sanctum

You know not the thoughts that are in my head,
you feel not the passions within my heart,
you read not the meanings deep in my soul,
you contain not the flights of my spirit.

My inner life belongs to me alone
so find that boundary, your line and mine
for the inner life is to be hallowed.
I have no need for you to cure it.

Philosophize how you may and then some,
socialize as you do; it matters not;
politicize those who live the inane.
My soul has its way; do not come near it.

Hallowed be the name of he who lives true
for the truth emerges from the hallowed.
Inner Sanctum waits for those who choose
to follow its call; fail not to hear it.

Cast me within your conceptual frames,
make believe you know me due to my faith,
think you size me up because I'm a man.
My Inner Sanctum lives. Heed or fear it.

Austin, March 2013

Highway Eighty-Four
(North out of Fort Sumner)

Highway eighty-four is etched in the land.
Except for an occasional screeching
of a hawk and a wolf's howling, the gods
quietness and stillness promote their reign.
Silence is a crystal born by the wind;
the silence is pure, the wind is spirit.
The wind whispers and brings forth the silence.
But the cries of the hawk and the wolf are
not discordant but belong to the land.
Like the tumbleweed and lambent sunlight
that move across the land like poetry,
like the crevices and the stark plateaus,
horizons that never appear to rest;
they all mark the foothills where they belong.
On that ground the highway claims existence,
bathed in silence and caressed by the wind,
generating no opposition but
lying in harmony with what is there.
The lone two-lane pathway speaks a language
expressing itself with no need for sound,
but beckons all to listen and be still.
It is in the land like wind and silence,
and sets with the gods and disturbs not how
quietness and stillness watch over all.

Austin, October 2013

road kill

right and wrong
in a protest song
radio stations
replaced by *Pandora*
plastic replaced by
tapes replaced by
digital everything
digital clock signals 4:57pm
going nowhere in a hurry
with nowhere to go
a sign that reads
no shirt no shoes no service
a billboard beckons
$495 round-trip: *Catalina Island*
nude beaches somewhere
in the world
getting away
getting back
to simplicity
a memory surfaces
about first love
a question haunts about
loving one's work
philosophizing about
loving life
glaring window shields
squinting eyelids

blaring horns
who listens
who mourns
are we all forlorn
a man holds up a sign
on a street corner
the end is not near – the end is here
Jim Morrison lyrics
run through my brain
as well as William Blake
and Aldous Huxley
books of poetry
come to mind
does it matter
if words don't rhyme
humming *parsley sage*
rosemary and thyme
old movies girlfriends
old songs and romancing
early college days
the graduate chasing paper
getting straight Kent State
Neil Young *Nixon's Army*
white room black curtains
taboo what have you got to lose
listen to me baby
go ask Alice
she owns a restaurant
napalm newsreels

the hovering sound
of helicopters
boot camp San Antonio
and all those dreams
more friends and more girls
distant thoughts about
what could've been
a feeling coming on
to write about it . . .
all

Austin, June 2015

Where *Deep Calls to Deep*

*Deep calls to deep in the
roar of your waterfalls
—Psalms 42:7*

I have not sought where
deep calls to deep.
I have worn the coat of trifling
even thinner through the shallowness
of my existence.

The selfish soul walks in shoals
far away from the roaring waters
where *deep calls to deep,*
those waters where life is nourished
in Spirit.

The deepest lie is the lie
of self-deceit that truncates spirit and
avoids where *deep calls to deep* yet
seeks to harvest truth from
grains of sand spread over cobblestone.

Austin, July 2013

The Bridge

*The dream is the small hidden door in the
deepest and most intimate sanctum of the soul.*
—*Carl Gustav Jung*

In a dream I was a lone traveler.
I knew no reason for my excursion
nor did I know where I might be going.
There are those who say dreams have no meaning;
some say we walk in dreams in need to search.
On my journey I came upon a bridge,
a looming behemoth stretching over
a wide chasm that formed a deep abyss.
Alone I walked the highway leading me
to the bridge's ascent into the clouds.
Moving without direction or intent,
relaxed but not necessarily calm
I noticed a road sign, *Exit all here.*
The off ramp luring I stopped to ponder;
the path that beckoned was clear but the bridge,
a huge structure hidden in clouds and fog,
suspended in mystery, likewise called,
pulling at me from the heavenly mist.
I focused on the bridge staring in awe.
Its unclear destiny provoked questions,
its unseen end led to hesitant doubts,
but heed not its call brought fear of regret.
Unsure I chose to bypass the exit,

feeling I could never again return.
As I walked the bridge's steep ascension
I saw below the neatly planned city,
that destiny to where the exit led,
where matching church steeples on each square block
grabbed at heaven but fell short of their mark.
I traveled on toward clouds, mist, and fog,
beckoned by a call from the other side.

Austin, November 2014

Darkland

Remember Him before the silver cord is
severed and the golden bowl is crushed
. . . the dust will return to the earth
as it was . . .
          —*Ecclesiastes*

I see the walking dead
empty souls
simulacrums of living.
I fear that I am among the
voided forms
moving across a darkened landscape.
Refusing to speak to and acknowledge one another
eyes glance and then retreat from contact.
There is a difference
between solitude and disconnection
between searching and aimlessness
between silence and deadness.

In this lost world
there are those
who have been made ready to follow a guru
who will offer the poison that
turns hearts and minds from what is real
as though truth can be summoned
at any time
at any point
made to pass some menial test that allows
anyone who would run from life to find sanctuary
in nothing at all.

Spirits are drowning in a gray techno-landscape
where wetness of tears fails to irrigate
the heart and soul for caring because
those who would care grow weary of giving
lost in the emptiness of the altruistic rule
spent
desiccated
fallen
taxed beyond measure
both of their ability and willingness to care.

Winter has come.
No one
misses the autumn
hopes for the spring
longs to rest in the warmth of summer.

Coldness permeates the land
where the sun is shut out
not because the light has no warmth
not because the light has no power.
The seed of darkness has taken root
yielding a harvest nurtured
not by the sun.

The home provides no sanctuary
the land is no longer cultivated
the child struggles for existence
the harvest rots in the field of insouciance.

And the pleas of the fallen drown
in their chosen silence . . .

Austin, December 2012

The Wind Blew

The cocoon forms and
holds existence
for some time.
I emerged then
the wind blew.

Immersed in living
I built on what I knew
the formal shield.
I felt settled but then
the wind blew.

Confronted by space and time
scarred by necessity of choice
protective layers formed.
I carved a path and then
the wind blew.

Standing in a new station
the fuse grows shorter
the anchor not weighted.
I live and life will go on like
the wind blew.

Silent running
time moves in whispers
corners turned

lessons lost and learned as
the wind blew.

Austin, July 2013

Night Caller

Don't you want to go for a ride
Now to the other side
Feels so good you can cry . . .
(Thomas/Karisson/Winnberg/Jonback)

As I walked home one evening at twilight
I noticed a figure following me
that was a shadow in the distant dusk
vanishing as I turned to confront it.
The encounter left me fearing shadows.
An ominous feeling haunting my soul,
I felt the rush to get home before dark,
and once there I sought to ease my unrest.
Later I heard a knock upon my door
but when I opened it, no one was there.
Fear gripping me I stood still in the night,
feeling a strange familiarity.
I spoke at nothing present, *Leave me be.*
An inchoate dread had begun to spread
and I sought to shake it off with a laugh.
My unnerved laughter proved no conviction.
I closed and locked the door craving to hide,
hoping to barricade myself from all.
'Round midnight a voice awakened me and
I peered at the dark and whispered: *Who's here?*
Convinced then that I was merely dreaming,
I rose wearily stumbling from my bed,
walked to the bath's basin to splash water

on my face to startle me back to life.
I saw in the bath mirror's reflection
a shadowy stranger in the hallway.
I drew a deep breath on what was to come,
darkness surrounding him I yearned for light.
I stood stern garnering enough courage
and I spoke falsely, *I know who you are.*
Emerging from fear, anger now surfaced.
I was determined to wait his response,
facing our reflections in the mirror.
The darkened figure stepped even closer
as if to let me recognize his face.
A familiar presence fell upon me
but the moment he cleared the shadow's edge,
he disappeared to leave me stand alone.
In the mirror I faced a lone image,
with fiery eyes glaring back into mine.

Austin, April 2013

falling on a page

there are words forming on this page
in front of you right now
(some would say they're actually
        forming in my head)
but my mind tells me they're not
actually formed until all of them
        fall on the page
of course my hands can erase them
(or is that my mind also)
and that's even easier these days
with computers and all so that
words can be deleted quickly
        rather than erased
which puts forth the image
in front of you that what's
written here was accomplished
seamlessly without any mistakes
or whimsical changes of my mind
manifested in the movement of my
hands not really my hands but my hands
on a keyboard that form the words
magically through electric impulses
but the electric impulses don't form
the words because my mind does
at least that's my understanding of things
and understanding comes through the mind
anyway all of this is to say that words are appearing

on this page right in front of you where they fall
from a mind to the page that is really white light on
a computer screen that no doubt one day
will be transferred to a piece of paper
that we call a page that is really a tree
which is weird to think about my words
are falling from my mind onto a tree
showing all that the mind can impact –
well enough of these falling words
there may be just too much impact
hopefully your reading of this falling did not
cause you to hit too hard because falling words
can do that sometimes other times they let you
land softly then still other times they don't let
you land at all they just keep you floating
wondering what the hell was it all about
such is the life of falling on a page –
my mind and hands need to check outta here . . .

Austin, September 2015

Ghosts

3pm in an afternoon's soft light
    ghosts sat at tables in a quaint café
        with empty stares drawn to digital worlds
            on voided faces voiceless for contact

Austin, July 2015

As Nietzsche Laughs

I

They I have heard know all about living.
They I am told know what values to hold.
They know our good if only we accept.
They are the ones to whom we acquiesce.

II

We face this life with hopes of achievement.
We want to live what we are called to live.
But when life gets in the way of living
we let the world chip away at our dreams.
Impassioned hearts set sail on destinies
and encounter storms that hinder their way:

      killers of the dream ready to deny,

      failures viewed inbred rather than lessons,

      conventional wisdom that tells us *no*,

      sweet dreams of reverence hijack our course.

To carve one's path is not easily done,
countless highways entertain the broken
lay beneath the cold sun where whimpers stir,
where spirits cry for what they have exchanged
for being all but who they truly were.
We're told all the reasons we can't follow
that destiny which calls from deep within,

so rather than pursue pathways we own
we bow before the oracle called *they*.

Still a question nags – who the hell are *they*:
      They readily seek to bind with their rules.
      They step forward to smother the spirit.
      They circumscribe paths we are to traverse.
      They seek to kill courage due to their fears.

My thoughts of *they* through some reflective time
has led blank verse to fall on silly rhyme.
To think of *they* we must laugh at their game
as Nietzsche laughs sounding forth a bold claim.
Sad *they* too sacrificed their innate dreams,
their passion crusted over writhes and screams.
And *they* hear the silence now in their time,
not of dawn's twilight but dusk when light dies.
We too can fall deep into herd-like *they*
so let us not judge lest we stray their way.
Their herd's path is an easy one indeed
but apparent ease leaves the soul to bleed.

Roads of destiny are ones we must cut.
Pray we not travel another man's rut.

Austin, January 2013

driving into midnight

the highway unfolds before me
as does the dark
streams of light come and go
i want to see the faces
behind the lights
but then would rather not
they remain
in their personal spheres
generating an impersonal feeling
that floods over me and
that i embrace in all its fullness
not wanting to let it go but
knowing there are other faces that
indescribably stream in the dark
eyes floating in a dream
somewhcre nowhere
certain of my going and coming
i am unsure
as to where i am going
and from where I am coming
i seem to be running
from something
from someplace
from someone
was it the life i thought i had
but never had
was it the dream i came to know

that turned to be the anti-dream
was it the realization that beyond the dream
there was nothing else and that the dream
was not all
it was made out to be
was it all
i didn't want to know
but nonetheless knew
was it all
i wanted to have
and in the having had it not
was it all
i wanted to live
but in the living
found no life
was it her
was it her words
the words we said
the words we should've said
the words we wouldn't say
couldn't say
even if we wanted to say them
was it the love that turned to indifference
was it knowing she secretly loves another
was it wondering if any of it even mattered
was it who i thought i was
realizing that i was not
who i wanted to be
and could not ever be

and didn't really want to be
i'm only waiting
for the answer of answers
that will never come
that evades capture
like the dark that unfolds
that keeps me
driving
driving
driving . . .
into midnight
waiting for a touch
the need to make contact
the need for another's touch
to know that my body is here
that my mind is sound
that i am real
waiting for someone's touch
that i don't want to feel
a touch
that will wake me up from a nightmare
that holds as its deepest fear
that it is not a nightmare
that i'm really here and
that i want to be here
behind this wheel
listening to the wind against the car
with unseen faces driving with me
against me

beneath distant silent stars
effulgence pitched against black
surrounded by the darkest moment of night
waiting for the dawn
that i don't want to come
the wheels against the highway
humming in my head
there is only the humming
only the
driving
driving
deeper into the nightfall
the fear and the comfort of nighttime
my mind spiraling deeper and deeper
from the light of day
i can no longer see
the light of day
i don't care to see
lost
waiting
moving
running
breathing hard
driving
the highway endlessly stretching out
as i search its end
that is no end
that i don't want to end
in the distance somewhere back in time

i left an existence
i'm no longer sure of
but certain of
wanting not to have left
wanting never to return
so i'm
driving
driving
driving
i feel the pull to keep
driving
driving
driving
waiting for a touch
i don't want to feel
waiting
waiting
for an answer
i don't care to hear
running
moving
breathing
driving
driving
driving
into midnight . . .

Austin, March 2013

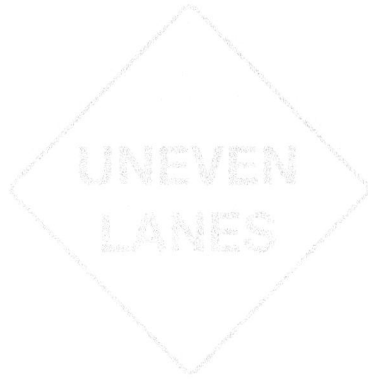

ANSWERING THE CALL

Anarchist

Searching for that space where the State is not
in nexus with time where politics die
where one's view of life belongs to one's self
the will to propagandize lies silent

and poetry evolves into its own.

Not that space where one wades shallow waters
nor where *the* questions are not considered
but a time where human minds are enriched
by contact with what lies far beyond them,

where *for the sake of freedom, freedom lives.*

Free from arbitrary powers that seek
to justify their existence where they
construct banal venues to keep in check
by their rules the wild at heart who live full,

engaging body, soul, mind, and spirit.

Austin, May 2014

The Machine

There's a storm coming
        and nobody knows,
from the horizon
        where a death wind blows.

When the thunder sounds
        words can't explain what
ominous risings
        will finally bring.

The machine well oiled
        others' fruit its health,
baptized in nostrums
        now reveals itself.

Upon fetid fields
        the will to fight gone,
the charnel now speaks
        worshipped as a throne.

Austin, October 2015

Words

Words, words, between the lines of age
—Neil Young

What are these things we call words?

These signifiers with power to sink into souls,
to embrace and wrap hearts with heat and chill,
to cure or sicken
wound or heal
encourage
destroy
strengthen or weaken
furnish life or kill.
They float in the air yet come from within.
We feel them all around us,
hear them in our head.
If spoken from those we endear,
they follow us like our shadow.
They may track us for a while
or may haunt us for some time.
They dance through the corridors of our minds,
like a puzzle play with memory and
turn our day on a moment's engagement.
By chance we encounter,

     a forgotten street corner
     a feel of the season
     a memory-filled tune
     a familiar face.

Lost words are triggered.
Suddenly we stand in
  a different time
  a different place.

These things called words,
we yearn to hear them yet fear their curse.
We anxiously wait
casting words in our head
that we hope or dread
will come from another's breath.
They are packed in conclusions
and pregnant with answers.
Within a fleeting momentary glance
they emerge from the depths of someone's eyes.
Words provide light or
they leave us in the dark.
We admire their gift of beauty and
fear their weight of pain.
They assure yet cast doubt.
They soothe but can scathe.
They reconcile
they separate
they reap
they sow
they cut like a razor's edge.
With them we calm a heart or
slash and bleed a soul.

Caught in the web of reflection on their power,
whether we've reached a clearing or
have fallen into a fog,
whether we're left suspended or
have stepped onto solid ground,
whether life is bred or
the damage done,
the timeless question never ceases to reappear.
Although an answer eludes our grasp,
indeed again
we must ask.

What are these things we call words?

Austin, January 2013

Exodus

I feel there are words
locked deep inside me
that want to get out .

(And they when set free
like waves of oceans
will flow without drought).

Austin, June 2013

A Poem

A poem might well tie you into a knot
with the thread of words that are a poem's lot.
But loosen the threads and what have you got?
A tighter bind by what a poem says not.

Austin, September 2015

We Seek

We seek the safety of not knowing
      only to bleed on the blade of what we don't know.
We seek the power of omniscience
      only to die by the dagger of what we think we know.
We seek comfort in anonymity
      only to be nicked by the knife of remaining unknown.
We seek the shallow depths of gregariousness
      only to plunge on the sword of being known but not known.

We seek the crowded streets of day
      to mingle with the faceless voided by the pain of living.
We seek the cover of night
      to hide from the light that illumines the path of living.
We seek that place behind closed doors
      to barricade our soul from the intrusion of living.
We seek the thick-walled sanctuary
      to retreat from the risk that is living.

We seek the horizon in the distance
      that calls us to break the bonds of thrown-ness.
We seek the rolling river called time
      that is wont to confine us to the flow of its existence.
We seek the cemetery bleached colorless by the sun
      that clarifies the universal destination.
We seek a name engraved on a stone
      that reifies and inflames this moment of being.

Austin, January 2013

Disciplines

Standing in the noise we miss the sounds of living;
staid in silence we hear a voice calling.

Basking in the crowd we lose our identity;
bathed in solitude we find our comforter.

Stained by voluptuous desire we always hunger;
steeped in fasting we are filled to fullness.

Wrought by the things of the world we find constant worry;
wrapped in simplicity we discover abundance.

Running with the rush hour we have lost our highway;
reclaiming our path we discover the way home that was always there.

Desperate in the heat to prove our worth we find a desert;
deliberate in the waiting we find a nourishing oasis.

Harried in the hurrying we run past the prize;
humbly in the calm but simple walk we find true wealth.

Austin, March 2013

What Lies Behind?

*We know the whole creation has been
groaning as in the pains of childbirth
right up to the present time.*
—*Apostle Paul: Romans 8:22*

When I look at the river
    and long to enter its rill
        when I hear the song
            in its purl

when I stand in the sun
    and bask in its warmth
        and lay beneath
            its afternoon charm

when snow-covered mountains
    fill the horizon to where I travel
        and they majestically
            rise out of the earth and hover

when a hummingbird quantum leaps
    from flower to flower
        indulging the sweetness
            of life they provide

when the bluebonnets roll
    and swell like an azure surf
        and turn a highway
            into an artist's canvas

when the grayness of the day
    sinks to the bone
        and pulls me
            toward that friendly melancholy

when the alpenglow
     lines the sky
          like a painter's brush
               reaching for the beyond . . .

There is a longing that calls
     one that I believe belongs to
          all of them and
               to all that share their realm
for upon reaching them
     touching and engaging them
          they fulfill yet supply only
               further pangs of longing
for in their beauty lies
     a sadness and an incompletion
          and a seeking that
               marks them as well.

Perhaps it is that
     which lies behind them
     for which I long
          for which I yearn
like a secret for which one's hands
     were never made to grasp
          the object of desire
          unfailingly slipping away.

Perhaps completion is an ongoing journey
    and what is incomplete will forever
        be drawn to an unseen
Mystery that clarifies and completes all . . .

Austin, January 2015

Grasping for Eternity

We cast our nets of perspective on time
to seine some sense of eternity
but it's not so easy a catch this sea of time
stretching beyond our concrete lives
demurring to explicate what's eternal.
Seeking false comforts in exigent acts
we cast in a moment's desperation
denying what desperation seeks to teach us.
Daunted not by the strength of our gray mesh
time bursts the nets of our categorical posturing
not to be hauled in like the day's catch
defiantly outlawing our percepts
refusing to be circumscribed by our smallness.

As we cast and strive
we find ourselves swept upon a Nantucket sleigh ride.
Time jostles
writhes
plunges
breaches
descends
takes us to the haunting depths of its being
allowing not our full comprehension
laughing at our sternness
cunningly escaping
the flimsy structure of our rationales.
Wrestling

teasing
tickling
it plays with our framework
and then tosses us back to shore
on the ground of our thrown-ness.
We are frightened at its taunting
its awe filling eternal soundings as
it circles back around allowing us
only a momentary glimpse into
its fearfully surveying eye
asking if we want more
teaching us to understand our place
to be more radically accepting than we are.

Ancient wise ones have already affirmed
a time for this and a time for that.
A time for
melancholy and tears
doubts and despair
hope and laughter
belief and joy
a time for the heat of passion
and a time to know
that eternity breaks the boundaries of time
possessing depths we cannot possibly sound.

The howling winds erase flowers from the fields
that for an instance claim existence.
The sands of time absorb footprints leaving

no trace of paths once traveled.
The seasons come and go
not asking permission from those who live within.
The galaxies continue their cycles
taking no special notice of travelers in space and time.

We do not capture the sea of time:
we are merely along for the ride.

The supercilious desire
to totally encase eternity
depicts not how large we loom
but betrays how small are our templates upon which
we stand and shake our hardened fists at the infinite
with demands of clarity as if mystery
would willingly and easily surrender its axioms.
Through the frayed and broken nets of our percepts
we face the foolhardiness of our desire
to extract from time our supreme importance
to reduce eternity to some time-bound explanation.
Through our frailties
we are set in the span of our finitude
not a vast sea but
a river of flowing moments
from which we draw meaning
only by confronting the mesh of limits that
time casts upon us.

Austin, December 2012

Corinthian Night

O Corinthian
night now

       showered by
       light of day

              your snake venom
              carries no pain.

Austin, June 2015

My Avatar

If I had to pick an avatar
      felicitous to my being
            the eye of silence
                  it would be one that must depict

A Night Wind furtively blowing
      through the living shadows of voices
            doors opening and closing
                  eyes gazing and turning
                      lips touching and parting
                            hearts hoping and hungering

Viewed in the wake of a darkened vision
      that is not inimical but rather some
            cryptic viewing formulating
                a taciturn comprehension.

Its silence heard only through words on a page.

Austin, June 2013

Writing on Time

It's 3:00a.m. on the dot
and I'm in need of a plot.
Pressure is on, deadline's hot;
some plots cut it, most do not.

In writer's block time does run.
Now ticks the clock 3:01.

Austin, July 2015

Moon-Pie

Once upon a time . . .
Moon-Pie took a risk and decided to break the rules one day
and went out for a stroll
covered with a smiley happy face
because he felt free.
Like the Wind blowing across the Sea
is how he thought his freedom to be
so he decided he would go see the Sea
just to see how free the Wind did blow.
When he arrived to the shore
three Mermaids were playing his song.
Sultry they were with their fish tales fanning
black and red and yellow hair flowing
voices enchanting from the tide
and their bare breasts glistening wet in the salty water.
The Evening Star watched all from on high
winking above the crest of the most distant wave
and the Wind howled . . .
I am free.

Moon-Pie floated across the waves
that the Wind stirred
and looking up he smiled at the Evening Star
who returned his smile with a wink that seemed to say
this is the way it should be, Moon-Pie; this is the way it should be.
So Moon-Pie turned left toward the West and the Mermaids sung . . .
rock-on – rock-on, Moon-Pie.

The sense and sound all around him
the Wind in his smiling face
the beautiful song from the Mermaids
and Evening Star so accepting
overwhelmed his emotions.
Suddenly he believed didn't deserve his smiley face,
that he should relinquish the freedom that was now his.
Against this guilt that vitiates the will the Sea rose.
It sounded forth its rage in all its Natural defiance.
Evening Star flashed in the distance
above the waves that surged in power and might.
A storm began to brew and
the Sea broke violently against the shore
where only those who refused to risk stood still.
All the rules that were made for breaking
became surd things from a lifeless venue.

So Moon-Pie kept moving on toward the West.
The Mermaids continued to sing in chorus . . .
keep-on rockin' – keep-on-rockin.'
The Wind cried out with the howl of a banshee . . .
I am free – I am free.

Austin, March 2013

seeing red

red with anger

red blooded

red headed

red hearted

Red Cross

red tape

red guard

red faced

red lips

red hot

red light

blood red

crimson red

ruby red

brick red

commie red

blushing red

fiery red

red eyed drunk

red barn

red truck

red fox

red rose

red dress

red shoes

red laced
red dime
Khmer Rouge

Austin, July 2015

The Calling

I

The day dawns . . .

with ululations and mingled cries of the struggle to separate.
We become aware not of our own volition that we have volition.
No forfeiture of the game
no abrogation of the scheduled destiny,
surrender never crystalizes into hard steeled reality.
The shield against life is avoidance.
Darkness is the home into which we are born.
The cold light of living penetrates
into the corridors of our framework
illumining paths set before and in time.

All comes with choosing and choosing not.

Awake.
The day is at hand.
Envision the battle that rages and will not cease.
We take what we are and forge what we hope to be into the forming
of an identity.
      One that will sound clear
            a clarion claim to all we value.
      One that will ring true
            a stark vision into horrifying caverns.
      One that will be and can be only in our being.

Hope against hope the war will not subside.
It calls for that is it what it does.
We heed so as to become who we are.
We heed not aiming toward being whom and what we are not.

We cannot not decide.

The metamorphosis evolves in pain
in love
      in honor
            in deceit
in bloody authenticity
      in honest tears
            in hope and desperation.
The path is set but not predetermined
unfolding
in choosing and choosing not.
Unconsciousness pulls at us to return from where we emerged.
It beckons us back into timelessness,
in the darkened desire
to forego who we are,
to forget where we have taken a stand,
to forfeit what we have declared,
to forsake all for which we have toiled.

Listen,
and you can hear the screaming of the fallen.

Can you hear
     the whisper
         the calling . . .

Heed not.
The calling does not cease.
     It burns.

Hear not.
The calling does not cease.
     It brands.

Care not.
The calling does not cease.
     It scathes.

Choose not.
The calling does not cease.
     It scars.

The calling does not cease.
     (I hear the screaming of the fallen).
The calling does not cease.
     It does not cease.

II

Reflect with me upon a time when time was not time,
when time did not matter in terms of time,
before time begat time in conscious recollection.

Recall those summers that stretched into seamless days
like batting eyelids
opening
      closing
            gone.
Batting eyelids of consciousness,
snapshots of time before consciousness caught and restrained time.

Recount a perceived eternity of winters with fresh frigidity,
frozen tree limbs reflecting the cold sunlight,
the anticipation of the thaw in warm embraces,
instilling memory with frames of time before consciousness framed time.

Recollect the feeling of eyes gazing with pleasure,
that first heating of blood speaking of the yearning
to touch
to know
to be touched
to be known.
Crossroads confront every life.
They tell an unconscious forgotten story,
how consciousness is formed in courage and fear,
carved in cowardice and lamentation.

Reminisce with me upon a time before time became time,
when new beginnings stood out of time ready to be formed
through first choices that laid the foundation that
turned timelessness into consciousness of time.
Timelessness set fresh

pristine
clean
ready to be casted upon a sea of time
soiled and tainted but necessitated by
conscious choosing and choosing not,
forming the burden of constantly sculpting an identity.

Why then do we fret in such feverous pitch?
What time is it?
When and how did I come thus?
My oh my where did time go?

The desire to retreat into timelessness
or to project time into endlessness
is one and the same.
Time,
conscious time,
is in the choosing and the choosing not.

III

I wanted to go back to the beginning of you and me
and
have it as it began when I first gazed upon you.
But
you said
      I remember you said
the changes come
and
there is now no more beginning.

There is only now.
The now that I chose was stained with weakness and lack of resolve
but
I wanted to go back to the beginning of perceived strength.
The now I chose with you was not strength
and
I continued not to choose strength
and
you saw that I chose it not.

I wanted to go back to an abstraction where I thought strength lived,
to be born
to be taken up
to be rekindled.
I wanted to go back so that I could say *this is who I am.*
But
the beginning moved into the now
and
I was what I chose in time.
The inauthentic wants the beginning after the hour chimes,
having recorded decisions
branded on the soul like a Scarlet Letter.

Strength lay in the future in that past if I had chosen it in that now.
It did not lay in the beginning because I did not choose it.

I wanted to be with you what I was not
and
you knew that I was not what I wanted to be,

striking out in anger,
>pain and weakness in anger and pain.

I wanted the beginning with you yet it had vanished.
>It did not vanish of its own accord.
>It did not vanish haply through arbitrariness.
>It did not vanish because of what you did and said.

But
because of what I did and said . . . and did and said,
repeating what I did and said again and again and again.
Cowardice and weakness lie in longing for an abstracted beginning,
nullifying that which has already ventured into the present,
unfolding not peradventure but by conscious choosing,
that in fear the spiritually lame hopes against hope
will retreat like sea waves from the shore back into unconsciousness.
What could have been with you lay in the future in that past now.
It did not lay in the beginning where I wanted to return where there
is no return.

Courage
lies in embracing the branding fire of present choosing.
If such choosing is held in disdain creating a different future
through
peregrinations along different paths
healing paths
strengthening paths
that confront and do not retreat from present choosing as though
the present
could resolve back into timelessness as if it were never consciously
chosen.

You said in so many ways,
        I remember you said in so many ways,
the human stain of living cannot be erased.
Perhaps to some degree it can be assuaged with a healing scar
but
never reclaimed by the beginning,
never it seems retrieved as not chosen.

This is the rhythm of the struggle with which we must become
conscious:
beginnings travel now in movement toward the future,
not to be reclaimed in a past that never journeys out into the now.
Housed in that yearned-for reclamation is a desired loss of
consciousness,
the hope of time before time not becoming time in choosing and
choosing not.

I remember what you said and the remembrance is with me now.
That my beginning cannot be resurrected as though there is no now.

IV

Arise.
The storm is on the horizon.
The never ceasing moment folding into moments
calls us to face the ominous clouds of
what we know we can't know until we enter the storm.
There is no peace
except the peace that comes through the war.
The coward evades the war

only to find its clouds hovering where he resides.
The storm beckons and calls because that is what it does.
We heed the call because that is what we are formed and set to do.
We heed not the call because we do not envy our form or where we
    are set,
thrown into a war not of our making but that is our making.

Negation of timelessness begets time.

The day breaks . . .
If we choose to heed
we have nonetheless chosen in the midst of unknowns.
If we choose not to heed
we have nonetheless chosen,
    in the midst of unknowns.

The path is unclear but that it is a path.
If we launch we journey as a voyager in the night.
If we yearn we yearn for what is hidden.
The emptiness that comes with surrender brings
regret
    doubt
        shame.
The failings that come with confrontation are marked with awe and
wonder,
those wonderful failings that come with the risk to engage.
We enter the storm;
    we hang back
    we surge forward

we slow our gait
we quicken the pace.

I hear wailing
crying
sighing.
      I feel the separation in the metamorphosis.

The calling
      the calling
            does not cease.

Can you hear
      the whisper
            the calling?

(I hear
the screaming of the fallen).

The calling does not cease.
      It inflames
The calling does not cease.
      It incites.
The calling does not cease.
      It incinerates.
The calling does not cease.
      It ignites.

The calling
    the calling
        does not cease.

It does not cease.
    It does not cease.

Austin, September 2012

Answering the Call

The time to change has come and gone
Watched your fears become your god
—Jerry Cantrell

Somewhere in the recesses of memory and time
an alarm rang loud yet soft
and through the silence of an inner monologue
I heard the words
someone's calling.
With every calling a question
surfaces
festers
perturbs
a sharp-edged pebble inside one's shoe
a stone against one's heel
a boulder cast upon one's path.

What if I answer . . .
What if I don't . . .

And the day turned.

It was a day much like today
sun angling through oak and birch trees
over concrete and asphalt
a warm afternoon
when the early evening had settled

into a pre-dusk comfort
a soft assuaging breeze that separated
the colder months from the
scorching ones to come.
Only
there was an alarm sounding
loud yet soft
aggressive but benevolent.
Someone was calling.
Only I could respond
no one else.

What if
What if I . . .

And the day turned.

In the weight of that moment
a world tugged on a life
a plangent sound
not vicious
not onerous
not destructive
but exigent.
There are decisions that make little difference
meaningful differences belong to some decisions.
I felt the calling would lead to turns along the way
birthing into life differences that would matter

because it pressed hard yet gently
softly upon me.
It emerged from memory and time.

The calling
sounded
executed
searching for wisdom's door
peering into inner caverns
to illumine false idols
of self-deceit
causing pain that is living
cutting through fear
coming to grips
pulling back
putting off
pushing on
toward what was known and unknown,
all that could not be known.
There is only
answering the call.

But what if
But what if I . . .

And the day turned.

Austin, March 2015

Returning the Call

Tell me what you plan to do with
your one wild and precious life?
—Mary Oliver

All the values on which you say you stand
but came not from what you searched out yourself
are not your own,
but are values that you inculcated
from others in time and then across time
but are not you.

All you say that you believe to be true
but did not come from your search for the truth
is not your truth,
but are thoughts and beliefs given to you
by others who sell truth you have purchased
but you own not.

All you claim in the name of who you are
that emerged not from the search in yourself
cannot be yours,
but are claims others have thrown upon you
so as to claim you for themselves whereby
you are not you.

All that guards you from owning who you are
will be exposed in the cold light of truth

as that false you,
but the scales that cover your eyes will fall
when you engage that soulful search to see
you as you are.

Austin, May 2014

REFLECTIONS
ON CYCLICAL JOURNEYS

Night Comes

Each day
night comes calling
and it falls,
falling
it engulfs
surrounds and consumes
the day.
Then there is the night.

Each turning
autumn falls,
winter descends and deepens autumn,
the days are a darker gray
and when night comes calling,
falling
it falls heavier.
The nights are longer and deeper.

Each breath
possesses as a gift its own light,
yours and mine,
but night always comes calling.
In kind across time it falls,
falling
this night is known only by the one
upon whom it falls.

Austin, June 2013

Restless

Darkness wrapped in doubt
      hovers over and rains down
            at the edge of existence.

Horizons unfold
      like waves in towering
            walls of water on a sea

Searching for calm
      hoping for rest
            from the unknown

Seeking to break
      through the edge of night
            to bathe in light again.

In the warmth
      there is rest
            there is calm.

Long in rest and calm
      the night wants in
            hovers and rains.

Beneath the sun
      the edge of existence
            never ceases to pull

Toward darkness
    wrapped in doubt
        into the unknown.

Austin, May 2017

7 Sounds of a Broken Heart

This is the sound of a broken heart
>   the cry of a wolf
>   over its mate that will never
>   return from sleep.
And this too
>   waves crashing
>   against a sea wall
>   in a hurricane.
This is the sound of a broken heart
>   the drip when
>   a teardrop falls
>   into a cup of coffee.
And this as well
>   a siren piercing the night
>   in a race
>   toward an unknown exigency.
This is the sound of a broken heart
>   the winter wind
>   howling incessantly
>   its disconsolate note.
And this
>   the door closing
>   when one's lover leaves
>   never to return.

This is the sound of a broken heart
    the deafening silence
    in what used to be
    a home.

Austin, May 2013

Too Many

Too many voided names, faces, and eyes,
      hearts and spirits swirl through life like silent
winds across empty plains blowing nowhere,
      essences denied lives unacknowledged.

Austin, June 2013

The Speed of Light

The summer heat
lies still over the day
though a small breeze
moves like silence.

The heat the stillness
the silence return my
thoughts to youthful
summer days

where life fully breathed
beneath the sun
evergreen and oaks
in formative years.

Instantaneously
the scene with emotions
emerges then recedes
into deep labyrinths.

Like the breeze memory moves
through a time in a place
I hope never to be
released

captured in an instant
by words
written on a
page.

Austin, July 2015

Cold Steel

Something in the soul
deep in your body
tells you it's coming.

The autumnal weeks
that followed the furnace
of June through August
precede its onslaught
from the panhandle
to the Midwestern Plains.

The next day's forecast
is merely repetition of
what your joints are
already letting you know.

The sun sets with a melancholy
red painted horizon that says
you're saying goodbye
to something though
tomorrow's fireball
will rise.

Bringing instead of heat
a northern wind emerges
with an edge of cold steel
that chafes and

burns the skin
slices and glides
through raw flesh
then sinks deep down
to the bone.

Austin, January 2015

Steel and Glass Winter

The gray day
forms a canopy over steel and glass
depletes the life-color of
buildings, city lights, billboards, and people
casting everything and everyone in gray.

The iced wind
brutally canalized through narrowed alleys
and shot down side streets,
suddenly opens upon parking lots and
swirls along nude plazas,
surges across vapid avenues,
spills over gray concrete boulevards
where it
cuts raw flesh
peels back eyelids
crystalizes teary eyes
draws faces downward
steals all forward vision,
heads bowed without prayer.

Those who predicate
winter's essence as passing
surely have not felt
the cold steel air in a still colder city
where there is a pervasive feeling
that nothingness wrapped in permafrost

has converged on steel and glass
and permanently stained all in gray.

Austin, June 2013

Ditty in Rapid City
(It's Still Winter on Easter Day)

I heard steel raindrops falling
I felt breezes wet and chilled.
The sun on clear winter days
never seems to find me warm.

I saw nighttime descending.
I listened to voices call.
Did not want to surrender
but my soul was turning cold.

Austin, October 2013

The Angry Rain

Who can be angry
at the angry rain
who will refuse
its mutinous hegemony
who stands to defy
its defiant threats
who prays to console
its disaffected darkness
whose heart is troubled by
its obstreperous winds

The rain rebels raging now where
drought promulgates dominance
where fire yields too often to the
tempting catalyst of dried kindling

Who can be angry
at the seditious force of anger
projected onto the rain
so as to propitiate the anger of
those already long-angered
with the reign of drought

Austin, June 2013

What I Believe When It Storms

The awful beauty of the thunderstorm
      is felt in the fear of hail pelting down
      on trees, shrubberies, planted flowers, and
      on parking lots, automobiles, and homes.

I sit comfortably in my study
      seeing that darkness has covered the day
      hearing the echoing thunder wage war
      on all that we hold dear beneath the storm
      and foolishly believe that I am safe
      so that I can listen to raging winds
      torrents of hail slamming against windows
      so I can look into terrifying
      power emerging from unknown sources
      feel its weight bearing down on existence
      and hear it move toward distant places.

Might these walls, weathered glass, tile covered roofs
      be metaphors in which we place our faith?

I hear the thunder now in the distance
      waging war there leaving calm in its wake
      and a feeling that metaphors are real.

Austin, May 2013

Rebellion

I hear the spring rains falling this morning
as they gently caress the hill country.
Now I sit staring out my bay window
at the thick black-gray sky full of moisture.
A morning dove coos, a gentle wind moves
through the pines and surrounding thick foliage.
The Austin hills are now lush with greenness
coming out of winter that left them brown.
On the trees, shrubs, and earth time signs its mark.

Behind me on a wall the second hand
of a clock sounds off that which we call time.
Disparately I try to cast the sound
on the dark spring day but it refuses
to be meted by the artificial.
Instead it sets a boundary between
what is and what tries to reduce what is
to our mechanistic understandings.
I soon find I no longer hear the clock.

Austin, May 2013

She
(if there's an age of innocence)

She
on a sun-filled spring morning
in a little pink dress and matching
bonnet dappled with white polka dots
in her awkward stage
exuding a bundle of energy
with inborn rebellion from
a lineage somewhere back
in time that will serve
her well throughout time,
breaks free from a guiding hand
laughingly escaping her bonds.

She
precariously stumbles
weaves sinuously across an open
rich green yard with an
innate courage from someone
she uses to explore her new world.

She
walks then sits
stands up
plops back down
undeterred

then for the first time
discovers lawn grass.

She
pinches it between
her stubby little fingers
then reaches for more
undeterred
then for the first time
discovers yard dirt.

She
likewise discovers that
both grass and the dirt
effortlessly can be
brought to her mouth,
a naturally innocent
thing for her to do but
hears one of those
big people scream
no
a word always to her disliking
evidenced by frown, scowl,
wrinkled forehead, scathing eyes.

She
nevertheless will hear
its reiterated command
at least a million more

times before she turns
five.

Austin, July 2015

The Sojourner

I am the sojourner.

I have driven the highways
    and the back roads
        floated the *friendly skies.*

I have stood in solitude
    on a silent solitary highway
        engulfed in deep quiet.

I have bathed in the sun
    swam an ocean to the horizon
        awed at the alpenglow.

I have read books
    studied the earth
        explored the mind.

I have struggled
    to tap into the heart of things
        and find rest with the Spirit.

I have gone down to the water
    washed in the shoals
        but feared the deep of the deep.

I have felt the clean crisp breeze
      been bit by howling cold winds
            stilled in silent days of no wind.

I have been on a mountain
      stood in a desert
            loved and lost the green hills of home.

I have pondered Time
      sought to choke the life from Time
            watched Time flow through my hands.

I have heard the questions
      repeated the questions
            pretended an answer.

I have run toward the light
      fearfully fled from the light
            willfully walked in darkness.

I have journeyed into several decades
      that I thought always lay ahead
            but the earth keeps turning towards a journey's end.

I am the sojourner.

Austin, February 2015

Soul Pathogen

we take a Pill to laugh but not too raw
    we take a Pill to judiciously cry
        we take a Pill to revive memory
            we take a Pill to forget then to die

Austin, June 2013

Death Fear in Iambic Pentameter

I speak to those who live in fear of death,
a fear that fills us all and steals our breath.
You may pretend that death comes not your way,
you take each breath and live from day to day.
Nor do you know your end when it may be,
so hide from death but still you are not free.
The life you're here to live you must live full,
but fear of death leads to a life that's dull.
Face up to what may come and don't retreat,
let not the fear of death bring your defeat.
It's not the fear you have that makes you wrong,
but how you face such fear stains weak or strong.

Austin, March 2015

The Grave of My Father

I stand above the grave of my father
      knowing that I too will lie in this ground.
He was a man who like all men wanted
      to live longer than his calling allowed.
He lived in strength and bore the weight of love
      dying at that time when time deemed it right.

Life is a felt wind coming and going
      turning with inexorable cycles.
Time is not inimical but measures
      how intrepid is our will and fervor.

How inveterate our velleity.

Austin, April 2013

Awake

I do not know why I am wide-awake.
I toss and turn while thoughts run through my head.
My eyes see the sun at horizon's edge.
I ponder why still I am wide-awake.

I hear the clock and its sound will not stop.
While my heart ticks and tocks in sync with time
I close my eyes and hope that rest will fall.
But still find that I am wide-awake.

I'm in a dream so sleep has come at last,
but not the kind of sleep that carries rest.
My dream fights to keep wakefulness at bay,
yet still I sense that I am wide-awake.

Morning comes and I find it's *all* a dream –
thoughts, dreams-in-dreams, clock, and horizon's edge.
I wrestled through the night and while I lay
my body found no peace nor did my mind.

For sure this is a mystery to me:
how one writhes in dreams yet is wide-awake.

Austin, May 2014

Terminal

The train pulls into the crowded terminal
where others wait with emotionless faces,
and through multiple doors springing open
we exit onto cold cracked concrete where
we scurry like roaches to our destinations.
We brush shoulders with those entering
but dare not acknowledge their existence.
Chilled dank air in the terminal forewarns us
of what is to come from the open streets.
Once we step outside bitter winds canalized
through avenues and alleys engage our being
like wind tunnels with the force of enmity.
Some of us hurry through swinging doors
into skyscrapers where the grind of daily
tasks takes hold to be repeated another day.
Others of us with tasks not so defined
run into coffee shops, breakfast diners
or Internet cafes regretting the long wintry
peregrinations we must follow to find
our place in this struggle we accept as life.

Austin, May 2017

Elixir of Life
(6:12a.m.)

The eructation of the coffee pot
    signifies a new day
        happy wakeful sounds
            that cause the blood to pump.

The swirling sound that the brew
    makes when being
        poured into a mug
            melodiously stirs a sleepy soul.

The scent of the black magic
    mesmerizes nostrils
        electrifies synapses
            summons taste buds to task.

The alchemy of water to grind
    is always the challenge
        chasing a taste equating
            to the glorious aroma.

Countless dreamers have told the tale
    should one perfectly capture
        such an evasive equation
            it must be packaged to

Bring peace, happiness, and nirvana to the universe.

Austin, May 2013

Promenade

The lawn had been wintered
brown and yellow in the promenade
surrounded by stone structures that housed
hotels, bookstores, and boutiques.

Yet a tuft of green protruded
in the center of the promenade yard
rich, lush, and alive,
calling attention to itself.

Although weeks remained in winter
the green-rich cluster and the surprising
visit of a seventy-five degree day
spoke of relief to come.

But now is the time to be
seven or seventy-five degrees
a hundred and five as it may be,
for autumnal visits during late-summer drought

had spoken as loud of relief to come.

Austin, January 2015

O Ephemera – Venustas Aeterna

Beauty lies in the strangest of places
green yellow and white bulbs
on a milkweed that becomes the energy for the
poor tiny caterpillar
we give the sad sounding name larvae and
like humans cut off from life do

We recoil from creepy crawler things.

While in the weird looking pupa,
the mysterious chrysalis,
amazing transformations even more mysterious
occur behind a wall of metamorphosis
that burst forth like flashes of gold and black light
in eternal return.

Beauty emerges seemingly ex nihilo.

I often wonder if the King passionately
seizes the life of
floating on the wind in effortless artistry
filling the fields with mesmerizing color
flooding the world with an awe of wonder and
seeks to live fully

His short reign upon the earth.

Austin, January 2015

A Late December Wind

I feel a late December wind that blows
    through the evergreens and bare-branched oaks
        signaling the end of autumn
            across the land.

It has blown here for eons of years
    at a time when I did not know its passing
        signifying beginnings and endings
            in its cyclical journey.

It will blow here eons to come
    inexorably along its sinuous paths
        singing the constant song of mutability
            across the land . . .

At a time yet again when I will not know its passing.

Austin, March 2013

Freeze Frame

Each moment that passes
      is that moment's last passing.
Each breath we suspire
      is that breath's last breathing.

Austin, June 2013

Tight Places

When you're in a tight fix
and you need a way out
but your vision is as far
as only human eyes can
see, then you need to
reach into your mind's
eye that can journey
far beyond the body's
vision. But when your
body is tired, worn, and
sore, all that weight tends
to hammer the mind's
vision so that it too falls
short. The tight feels
tighter, the way out looks
smaller, closing all around
you, and turns dimmer with
each glance. Sometimes you
find a way out; other times
you do not. Sometimes you
feel the wind, and the
strength in your body returns
just at the right moment. Other
times it goes differently and you
sink in a dank existence. This
occurs so that you can mark
your way with wins and losses

about which only you know
the difference.

Austin, May 2017

The Hunter

I sat comfortably one cool fall morning
before sunrise on a balcony at a bed and breakfast
outside Kalispell ready to hike for the day.
I sipped hot coffee from a thick steaming mug
clinched tightly to warm my hands while
sitting peacefully waiting for the sun.
I heard an eagle's cry fill the morning sky.
I searched desperately to catch a glimpse of
the magnificent creature like many that fly
around the glacier but darkness covered all,
not allowing the human eye to break the dusky cover.
I listened and heard its cry again and then the
third cry broke the silence with a long shrill.
Then I saw the reason for its joyous call.
Morning's light just then peaked over the mountain
as the creature spoke to the power of the sun,
which he could see upon high before any human eye.
Light had broken the night first for this powerful predator.
The hunter was ready to quest for another day.

Austin, August 2015

Wind and Spirit

The Greek language uses the same word for wind and spirit.

Some understand an owl as the spirit of a tree.
The call of a whale sounds forth the spirit of the sea.
Some believe an eagle's path discloses the spirit of the sun.
Others believe a quiet purl defines the spirit of how rivers run.
Distant echoes of beauty form the spirit of a mountain.
Hard pressed is one to exact the spirit of a human.

If the wind is the spirit of the world
    it blows where it wishes and is
    the breath of life for all of them.

Austin, September 2015

Actualities

I did not want to
believe
that
I am this person
the kind of
person
I hoped never to become
because it's so embarrassing.

I had just
graduated with a
master's in literature
and now
was going on three
months
behind rent.

I had a couple
of notices from
the apartment
owners
that lay crinkled up
in front of me
on my reading desk.

I knew then and there
I had to make contact

plea my case
look and feel
pathetic
like I knew myself
to be.

I sat in front of her
and
mentioned a job
that fell through
because of layoffs
and
that I would do
whatever
it takes to
make it
right.

She listened intently
understandingly
empathetically
compassionately
and said in an
affirming tone:

People just don't seem
to know how their
decisions affect others,
do they not?

I know you'll make it
right.

Bukowski
called these experiences
actualities
ones I prefer
not to undergo
because they feel shameful.

But then
here I am
writing about this
fortuitous event in
my life

as though somehow
in some strange way
as only living pulls off

it has informed
me.

Austin, May 2017

Reflections on a Cyclical Journey

I awoke
at a point in time
saw the sun rising
peaking over the horizon
its warmth radiating
my body throughout.
It was then
I knew the light of day
how the wind, clouds, and
flowers in the grass fields
engaged my body.
I heard the sound of an eagle,
took a deep breath,
through my veins
blood surged.

I stood fast in the heat
looked toward
the sun at high noon.
It appeared an old friend
who had always been there
when I needed light
warmth and comfort.
I breathed deeper,
my body full of strength
I watched the eagle
fly across the sky

in front of the sun.
I heard its call
echo the sound
of life.

I observed and felt
the enclosing dusk.
I began to think
somewhere
somehow
I was losing an old friend.
The breeze had cooled,
the cry of the eagle
had silenced,
all around draped
a dull canvas of light,
hard and fast fell the night.
In the place of the sun's heat
there appeared icy
starlight.

My body shuddered
like a lone leaf
clinging for life to its bough

in a wintry wind.

Austin, May 2014

These Hands

These hands that I scan right now,
these nails with their personal lines
brought on by life tasks folding into age,
these fingertips with their unique patterns,
this skin that I know is replenished in time,
all seem to have been with me always.

This freckle just below one knuckle,
the mole just outside the web between
my index finger and thumb. This
physical entity that I came to call me,
a friend that I don't want to lose but
one day will fade like physical things do.

I am here, anchored, grounded to this
physicality that I can come to
know if I choose, yet from which I
can so easily become disconnected.

I scan my hands and arms then run
my palms softly across my face, eyes,
and forehead – then use them to push
back what little remaining hair I have.

Take a deep breath –
I am still here.

Austin, September 2015

Frogs

I typed into the slot on *Bing*
Why do frogs croak?
We know that frogs croak.
We know the different types
of frogs. We can name them
in our biology classes for good grades.
Expert mimes can copy their sound
and we laugh thinking it's comical.
But why do they croak?
Are they thinking thoughts like
I need to croak right now?
Or is it a phenomenon that's
natural and determined and all
of a sudden a croak just pops out?
I hear their sound on the lake
usually after dark thickly falls.
Their sound is easy and pleasant
bringing peace and calm to the night
a feeling that you lean back into
and let it hold you like a thick pillow.
Maybe that's why frogs croak.
It's what they have to offer the world.

Austin, May 2017

Today

We glance back at memories carved in time
      easily snared by those kind and unkind.
            Forward we look but it's too far to see.
              Today is here so why not let it be.

Austin, August 2014

PRESENCE
AND ABSENCE

Avenue

I'll wait in this place
Where the sun never shines
Wait in this place
Where the shadows run
from themselves
—*Jack Bruce/Peter Brown*

A sharp edged winter morning finds us on
the avenue outside our secret place
facing one another in the cold light
that angles across city streets chasing
away lingering remnants of night in
which we became entangled in short lived
passion that fled from the dawn and the risk
to love.

A question haunts the shallow play we stage
disturbing that false but sweet delicate
balance that upholds our torrid game where
words are withheld for fear of becoming
known on a deeper level that beckons
yet sounds a cold warning knell that mimics
our scene that is our winter which we choose
to live.

Your eyes speak *do not ask any questions*
your touch mandates *we have only the night*
and your body grown cold with the morning

precludes congruent paths for you and me.
You then softly touch my face with your hand
and as your sad smile begs silence for now,
you shun a final embrace and then turn
to leave.

Austin, October 2013

Imago

She was a shock to the system
that I never overcame.

Body wrapped in rhythms
eyes with windows that beckoned
an image that I imagined
tapping into ethereal realms
making her an object of desire
severed from connections to roots of life.

She was a composition on a canvas
representing daydreams of enchantment.

Lips that soothed in tones
sensually fluid motions
hair that was tamed naturally wild
grace in movement like a muse
making her an apogee
guarded by categorical imperatives.

She was a position for which I stood
that never borrowed on practicality.

Dreaming dreams that we hold onto
for the desperation in dreaming
holding hopes that we cling to
for all the doubts in hoping

making her a vision of angelic splendor
suspended in clouds far above soiled existence.

She was a projection of my mind's eye
that never dared release her from the Forms.

Austin, August 2013

Addiction

And it's been awhile
since I could stand
on my own two feet again . . .
  —*Lewis, Mushok, Wysocki, April*

I found my way out of the night again.
where sunlit days began to lose their gray.
The air I breathed was clean once more.
My body having become less infected,
demons retreated one-by-one.
My brain aligned with what I perceived.
Step-by-step I exited my cavern,
stood beneath the purifying rays of the sun.
Against the staleness that marked my way of living,
I turned the corner to find a crisp fresh edge.

All of this came true for me
until I heard your voice again.

My nerve endings were no longer on fire.
My flesh had ceased at last to crawl.
The pain between my eyes began to fade.
I no longer waited for the hammer to fall.
The harshness with which I stared into the mirror
softened to a sober acceptance.
The stains on my soul began to clear;
I washed away the foul taste of bitterness.
Feeling ready to walk among the living,
I rose to face the destruction I had rendered.

All of this came true for me
until I saw your face again.

Candle light vigils
burned for my benefit
enkindled by those who had known
my before and after.
The separation having cleansed
finally a spirit emerged
where there had been
no life at all.

Because you were my life
you were my life sentence.

I found my path back to the sun
where I hugged and kissed the light.
Instead of disease my heart pumped blood,
the antidote to the poison that was my tongue.
My body healed and my mind found its path
back to its *raison d'etre*.
I played the court jester much too long
so I broke the ties that defined me.
Shattered pieces scattered over time
began to reassemble becoming whole.

All of this came true for me
until I fell into you again.

The wind blowing
through the candles
the flickering fire
could not be sustained.
Together we are
an addiction
tainted with toxicity that only
the jokingly cruel call love.

Because I made you the end of life
you were my end of all living.

Austin, August 2013

lost

lost
in the night
of her existence
into her darkness
plunge headlong
lost

Austin, June 2013

HeartDeath

Oh woman of the night
you had a candle of light
in your heart. And in the
coldness of my doubt
I snuffed it out.

Austin, May 2017

This Place

I'm waiting on the edge of town . . .
—*Greaves, Lister*

I traveled days on weeks to reach you here,
this place where you exist that no one knows
this place where neither maps nor road signs lead
this place that many have christened nowhere.

Here time has covered all the forsaken
where isolated hearts seek their solace
in deserted boulevards they have paved
full of emptiness beneath cold starlight.

This place I have entered without welcome.

Without mercy all seek silent-sleep here,
this place sets soundless, words priced valueless
this place tongues cry mute, faces stare eyeless
this place none seek warmth, bodies shun contact.

Here all live who have journeyed to forget
that betrayal by those to whom at one
time they entrusted the key to unlock
the door that had remained shut to others.

This place sets out of reach from all living.

I know you believe that I am the one
who took your trust, betrayed, and deceived you.
Now I ask you to trust this one last time,
to believe that *I will not let you down.*

I have long-journeyed hoping to free you
to lift you from this grave you have chosen
for yourself and all you hold to be true.
I am waiting for you till sunrise comes.

Waiting till sunrise . . . then I leave this place.

Austin, January 2015

Note Well

I had a life
now I have strife
just because
I got a wife.

My time was free
just for me
now consumed by
matrimony.

The end is near
I've lived in fear
because I called
someone *my dear.*

n.b.
(Whosoever
of you
seriously contemplates this poem,
poetry can prove no noted benefit
to you
whatsoever).

Austin, July 2013

lovelock

arms embracing
legs intertwined
bodies entangled
heat summons heat
breasts against breasts
heartbeat on heartbeat
face to face
minds in unison
rhythms of fantasy
souls bleed
one into the other
sprits enmeshed
unified in being

Austin, December 2014

My Bacchae

I saw her pic pop up online
remembered the things about her
that neurons tend to capture.
The way she dressed that revealed
all her lines and curves,
the way she moved in sensuous tones
a fluidity of motion and rhythm,
a presence that bespoke of intimate
familiarity and friendship
with the wildest carnality.
Full lips, jet eyes, sun-colored hair,
a body that yearned for seizing and touching
that called out to be known in frenzied ways
that beckoned fantasy upon fantasy
of falling, rolling, writhing,
scratching, thrusting, clawing,
crescendos in screams of ecstasy.
Fantasies of the body
in the spirit of the Bacchae and the rites of spring,
that Dionysian anchor to the earth
that is lost on many
who live largely in the world
of Apollonian designs.

Austin, January 2015

I do not know your name

Your touch is like a mystery
generating strange vibes
rhythms of your beckoning.

Your breath in my ear
warms my body
chills my soul.

You are a longing that
heightens my desire
fills me with a sense of perfidy,

You are a danger that
entices, excites, kindles
the fire of death.

Eye to eye
heart to heart
thigh to thigh
passion is your art.

Yet
I do not know your name.

The smoothness of your skin
is a magnet to
unknown sensual realms.

Your mellifluous tongue
yields nectars that sweeten the risk
to fall into you forever.

Desire folds upon desire
generating burning coals
the fire in your jet eyes.

A fire that promises comfort
yet consumes all
upon engagement.

Body to body
heat to heat
ashes to ashes
there is no retreat.

Still
I do not know your name.

Austin, January 2015

The Road

We chose the road that we wanted to take,
traveled it for a distance, claiming it
as a path that would always be for us.
Like so many roads, inroads, and outlets,
unseen obstacles arose on our way
toward that life we hoped to call our own.

After awhile we turned back on our road,
discovered how miles could not be undone,
saw too how our road could not be retraced.
We had made our choices along the way,
choices that cut paths not open to change,
for roads never surrender hard-fast truths.

Once traveled footprints are carved forever,
beneath the sun, in the dust, on our soul.

Austin, August 2015

This Green Hill

I lie alone on this green hill in
a lush field, a sea of green
feeling the soft grass against
the back of my head and arms,
the sun's warmth flowing over me
looking into a crystal blue sky
with soft white clouds gently
floating by in a softer breeze
cooling against the light sweat of my body.

I have lain here before with you so
I willfully drift into the flow of memory
but many would contend it's not the same,
not the same day, not the same clouds,
not the same grass that changes from
season to season, not the same sun
a star burning out with time,
not the same me, not the same you.

Here on this spot nonetheless
memory holds and clings to
a different time, a different season,
then too in the warmth of the sun
feeling the coolness of a gentle breeze.

I step back in time to that different life
even if just for a little while knowing,

although changes have come and with
them a new life has developed here, I,

on this green hill lying back in the grass
below the sun and bluest of skies in the
softest of breezes with slow moving
white clouds passing above like time itself,

choose to fold then into now
as though they are the same.

Austin, August 2015

You Will Never

You will never know my pain
hear the thoughts I hold
feel the razor blades that protrude
from my soul with which I cut a
path to where and how I need to go.

You will never see what lies
behind my eyes that filters and
voids what enters so the road I
travel runs smoother than it
really shows in the light of day.

You will never understand
how I formed this self and
what I came to be only in part
through who you are and
how you chose to live.

You will never walk the paths
I have followed
touch the ways
I have chosen
to live.

You will never surmise
how small the hand you played
in it all.

Austin, September 2015

151

The Siren

When your melancholy looked into me
I felt the weight of your gray existence
reaching out for someone to hold onto
seeking a lifeline over an abyss.
Falling, falling I dove into fathoms
feeling the strength of your downward spiral.
My fall had begun with one end in sight.
Your countenance drew me to your cold pain
where I longed to be the one who saved you,
retrieving you from the depths of sadness,
being that strength on which you set your course.
I plumbed deep to the shadows of your night,
down the labyrinth from where you beckoned,
diving into the hell of your sad eyes.
I wanted to understand your beauty,
longed to measure the expanse of your gaze,
to explore the mystery of your soul
that spoke in such disconsolate whispers.

I did not know nor see whence you had come.
Your mother was Gaea rising from earth,
bones of the dead surrounded your lair.
Like Odysseus who bound self to mast
I should have bound self far away from you,
closed my ears to the callings of your song,
a melancholy song of enchantment
beckoning me on to a chosen end.

Time and time and more time chose not to prove
that I was the fool I chose not to see.
Eyes with a leer that could not be refused,
the tears you shed formed your web of deceit.
The game had begun and the snare was set.
You were the one who cried out to be saved,
you who captures those who come near your call.
Your cries pierced the night like a siren wail.
I plunged into your mesmerizing hymn,
and in the plunge I discovered your trap.
The freshest notch on your weapon was I.

My fall began in response to a gaze
when your melancholy looked into me.

Austin, February 2013

Memorial to a Muse

I stood staring at the end of the day
where the line between late and early falls,
pondering my fate at the loss of words
that I could no longer find within me.
Desiccated, dried, empty of passion,
thoughtless, formless, lifeless river of death
flowing through my veins generating naught,
Poesy lost while I longed for her return.
I had fallen upon a dry season,
vision's well, once full of deep waters turned
to mud, with faint hope, finally to dust.
I hit that invisible wall yet one
so palpable it smothered my spirit.

You like a muse walked across my life's path.
I had never seen nor spoken to you
but you stood before me like memory
resurfacing in a lost emotion,
like a past lover now reappearing,
warming my soul in a sudden deep breath.
Dark hair gently lifting in a light wind,
darker eyes piercing long the cold distance,
wearing a black dress against the midnight,
in which we stood, surrounding you and me.
On that street in front of the old hotel
I watched you move in space and float through time

with mastered ease as though you ruled the night.
Your mystery so easily summoned
watchful eyes mesmerized by poetry
that enlivened the darkness of midnight.
Music emerged from your sensual moves,
eyes quickly glancing then turning away,
leaving me to wonder was contact made,
or would you slip through my grasp to nowhere.

Polyhymnia knows not your passion.
Euterpe with flute cannot play your song.
Even Clio with the great scroll of time
would long for the heat that you bring to life.
I knew as you walked away in the night
Erato had to be your secret name.
I found no sleep those hours before dawn,
your shape dancing through my mind like the breeze
that gently lifted your hair, leaving me
longing to know the softness of your touch.
I could not shake the pain of wanting you,
though all I had were those fleeting moments
of watching you glide through life like Poesy.
But all was not lost; for a muse you were,
stirring passions that lifted the languor
that had ensnared my mind like opiates.
On the wind you drifted before my eyes,
kindling a dry, dead spirit lost for words.
I knew you had become my sacred muse.

Many days after our short encounter
thoughts flowed free like a turbulent river,
lost words surfacing from a cold graveyard,
coming to life and flooding a blank page.
What I had lost our crossing had revived.
Poesy returned with verse filling my head.
Some I captured, some I threw to the wind.
What had become bankrupt turned to surplus
and I took some of the bounty and formed,
however it fares with critical eyes,
this memorial I hope you will read.

And if so I hope this thought comes to you:
I would long that such words be penned for me.

Austin, February 2013

Vampire's Ode

I come to you in your sensual bed
in this night which is my time for living,
desirous not to drain you of all life
but to offer only a slight puncture,
so that you can come with me forever
and join my journey into these nights
where we will rule while other spirits sleep.

Fear not the transformation that will now
open for you a forbidden gateway
to a universe you have never known,
one that will bring to you a new hunger
that you and I will quench eternally,
traveling the world in nocturnal bliss
where you will be mine forever to keep.

Fear not, fear not, you will be my lady,
my queen who rules with me beneath the stars
in a kingdom where sunlight is not known,
where we are awakened from deep slumber
when others lock their doors for the eve and
we then rise in flight to our dark calling,
fleeing crosses that send us to the deep.

Austin, March 2013

Let . . .

Let me bind flesh and bone with all that's yours
        let me see that place so deep that you guard
        let me smell the sweat of your skin in heat
        let me taste your fire that lies pure and soft
        let me sense your core move with mine as one
        let me speak the words your blood yearns to hear.

Let me take you where to risk is to live
        let me gaze in your eyes to find your soul
        let me know the depths you choose to lay bare
        let me feel your tears on me when you cry
        let me have all you want and hope to give
        let me through your walls so I may come near.

Let me be the call that draws you to seek
        let me be the safe place to which you cling
        let me be the hope for which you have ached
        let me be the wind on which you will sail
        let me be the mark you set hard and true
        let me be the ground where you cast your fear.

Austin, October 2013

Cold Bright Day

The shear brightness of the sun-filled day
appears an invitation to bathe in warmth,
but step outside from the comfort of this
cozy coffee shop, the bite of cold will
sink to the bone and instantly ice the soul.

I sit here in this reprieve impervious to the
chilled window through which I watch
people pass bundled in heavy gear,
guarded muffed ears, unknown faces
wrapped in scarfs with hooded heads,
cold stinging eyes forced downward.

You passed by this very window one
summer morning, I smiled at you, and
we began one of those strange fortuitous
events that opens doors that didn't exist
until that peradventure moment of
intersecting crossroads that led to an
unpredictable set of circumstances.

Now the icy wind rattles the window
so I can't escape this present winter.
I note the exhaust from automobiles
hitting and fogging the wintry air
mixing with condensed breaths that

rise softly like irretrievable words
carelessly cast onto a cold bright day.

I long for the warmth of that summer.
I do not want to walk outside alone.

Into the cold.

Austin, May 2017

Question

Is this a cold existence?

Your warm body counters that notion,
but your burning empty eyes bespeaks
a different tale, one that I have studied
over and over again, and one I would
rather keep at arm's distance from my core.

The fire stored in your soul made real
in the heat from your breasts and the
flames that run the length of your nakedness
speak of no winter here, but darkness hugs
the humid room in which we find ourselves
working out our separate details.

In my haze I feel a light trying to break through
but I am not sure what it is or from where it comes,
what words it hopes to bring here so as to rekindle
a mind that questions but evades the threat of answers,
shuns the fear of denouement.

Lying here with you is a reprieve from a sense
of stark madness that comes with not wanting
to engage or to encounter, a momentary pleasure
that covers nothing for very long, that fills no heart
with hope or grants no touch of what is real.

Is this a cold existence?

Your inflamed skin covered in beads of perspiration
screams *never* but only for a momentary grasp at
what could be, what is not, and what will never be
in dark, dingy rooms cached in timeworn, stone slab
buildings behind opened screened windows that beg
a cool breeze to enter just beneath the hot glow of
cadenced neon lights.

Austin, May 2017

In the Presence of Your Absence

In the presence of your absence
I feel the longing
that crept into the space you left in your leaving,
a longing
entombed in empty rooms, silent spaces, colorless existence
where voices echo words never spoken in their proper season.
We did not speak our desires and fears
but hid them in the void of silence,
not the silence in solitude where one gathers clarity
nor the silence in strength where one garners courage
but the silence of fear where cowardice generates soundlessness.
Yearning to speak my yearning
longing to voice my longing
I held my words like a miser clinging to
what possesses no value in the keeping.
Avoiding the heat of touch
angered at my fear of the fire
fearful of losing all
I froze in time to keep time from doing what time does.

Words
I did not speak that would have filled you
you did not speak that could have touched my depths.
Desiccation seized our being so
I listened for words frightened of withering
hoping for fullness without surfeit but

sounds came neither from your voice nor mine.
Words that strike to the core can bind or cleanly scalpel,
words that are reined in generate distance.
Binding calls for explorations into challenging depths,
the scalpel's healing cut scars but
etches lessons into one's being.
Distance measures the span of the refusal to risk
by words gripped tightly in a coward's remorse.
My speaking-not aimed not at shutting you out,
I did not withhold words to alienate.
I pleaded silently for words that did not come
yours and mine
leading me to travel deeper into silenced self.
I watched separation grow
while chasms widened and
in your speaking-not
I pictured you
drifting on great excursions of your own
leaving me in the measure of my quietness.
I longed to reach out to mete the length and depth of your drifting
but
I stood still
mute
closed to movement and sound
pregnant words never uttered
silence ruling.
I watched the perceived drifting turn into distance
fulfilling the prophesied fear.

Partings tell a story that must be told that in the telling
reasons crystalize into limpid pools of clarity.
Sitting alone with one's quietness
silence is accused but silence is a choice.
Who chooses . . . what . . . why . . .
what words explain the absence of words?
I can only reflect now that perhaps you felt the same as I
but I will never know because
we remained voiceless.
The risk of words is in the binding,
the risk of words is in the healing cut,
the risk of silence is in the distance,
the risk of risking carries deep-seated fears.
I wanted to speak to your fulfillment of me
to the beauty of your being
to your warmth
to your touch
to your softness
to your heat
to your living.
I wanted to speak to all of you.
I wanted you to speak to your measure of me
to speak to all of me
but I heard only silence,
yours and mine.
There lies in the future of speaking and not
the binding, the scalpel, the distance and
speaking-not *is* speaking.
I am surrounded by distance.

Being the authors of our fate reifies to this concreteness: You and I.
You in a distant life that is now your own.
I, in silence, living
in the presence of your absence.

[This poem was inspired by the music of Claus Ogerman and Michael Brecker and a long piece in three parts they wrote for their recording of *Cityscape,* called "In the Presence and Absence of Each Other."]

Austin, December 2012

166

Just Like You

Through a large glass front of a coffee shop
bright cold sunlight, a winter's afternoon,
freeway beneath the sun, unknown drivers
fading slowly out of sight – just like you.

Black coffee, white cream, damp spoons on saucers
stained napkins, framed moments of reflection,
thoughts rise calmly with steam from palm-gripped cups,
then vanish on waves of time – just like you.

Left alone with words whispered to oneself,
melting ice, tepid water, sharp-edged tings,
coffee spoons stirring pools of memories,
visions of evanescence – just like you.

Austin, April 2015

Ruing the Day
(But Not Really)

She said she was a muse
>	but it turned out to be a ruse.
Now my ego is bruised
>	'cause all my poems have been refused.

Austin, September 2013

SOMETHING ABOUT MIDNIGHT: (PROSE POEMS)

Dalliance

A couple of hours passed noon on a Friday and classes were done for the week. You came walking, smiling, across my yard toward the wood-framed box that was called a house that I had rented for the school year. I noticed the lines of your body through the short cotton dress you wore as you approached in sensual tones, your reddish-blonde hair flowing like fire in the sun as you moved. I had talked to you before, wanting to know you better, so your peradventure passing my way fulfilled my hope.

We bathed in early April's afternoon sun, sunk in beanbag chairs on my front porch welcoming the spring's warmest day. We had a couple of beers, we spoke of art, beauty, world affairs, love, and past relationships. In the middle of my living room floor we sat in lotus positions, shared a joint, and you talked in riddles, making me guess their meaning. When I made outrageous interpretations we laughed so hard our ribs and stomachs ached. (Later we would wonder why what I said seemed so funny.) Within the span of only a few hours, we fell into each other's gazes. We made love in the afternoon and napped.

Upon waking we drove to the best fish place in town where we devoured catfish and French fries. We would catch each other's glances across the table and giggle as we stuffed our faces with food without uttering a word. After the meal we went for a walk and talked about our favorite movies. Your list ranged from *Casablanca* to *Breakfast at Tiffany's*. Because I was a man (I thought) growing up in east Texas, my list ran from *Key Largo* to *The Wild Bunch*. I talked about the Hemingway formula and never breaking the code one lives by. I wanted to impress you with my prowess. That night we went to the theater on the town square to the opening of *The Godfather*, and you hid your face on my shoulder during its most violent scenes. You screamed when James Caan's character was assassinated on the causeway.

After the movie, we lay in each other's arms the rest of the night, dallying in the middle of the living room floor. In the still darkened early hours of morning, I awoke. Your body lay totally relaxed against mine. I pulled back the light blanket we used because the April evening had grown cooler, and I gazed at your nude form. You felt warm. I listened to the rhythmic cadence of your breath. I glanced toward one of the living room windows and caught sight of the stars through a slant in one of the mini blinds. I gently caressed you, you slightly moaned, and I drifted back to sleep.

Austin, June 2013

Isabelle Hardy

Isabelle Hardy tis' the name
Irish by birth
American by spirit
I've carved out my life
So don't you come near it.

For many years she punched the keys on one of those ancient cash registers that tinged and echoed throughout the Irish Café. She, an ornament framed within a day's juncture behind a counter conducting a transaction. One who greeted and was greeted in passing while the greeters moved on through life.

Belle, what is the damage done today?
Indeed tis' damage you say?
Oh, you know you like to pay
And leave me a good tip for the day.

I remember her only with gray hair tinctured red, a face that smiled but hid a melancholy tune, her leathery skin displaying the wear of time, the heat of worry, a longing heart, shades of sadness, one whose spirit seemingly soared but remained hidden, placed in space and time with no history. Her eyes would still twinkle when she heard a compliment or two.

The soup was delicious today
The roast melted on my palate.

You know I'm the best cook around
(she would boast with a hearty laugh)
But don't tell your wife
I know how to take care of you soul
Or should I say your stomach?

As happens with dull-minded youth, years turned before upon reflection I wondered about her life. Until then she was merely *Belle*, a fixture with a slight Irish brogue, the little old lady on whom we would cast jokes, tease about her funny accent when she expended effort to talk Texan; gibe her about her heavy made up face with thick, dark red lipstick and cheeks that looked bruised with purple rouge. Now and then in a light-hearted moment we would hear:

Isabelle Hardy the full name would boom
Says it's time to close.
And she would clear the room
and lock the door.

Then one day as I paid my ticket, I saw a deeper sadness in her eyes. She pointed to a picture behind her on a shelf as she had done a number of times as though this day and hour was her time to draw on memory. And I, at the register, wanting only to pay felt unlucky to be caught in her reminiscence.

That's my late husband. His plane went down you know.
Somewhere over Normandy.

I did know because I had heard the story too many times, but I nodded politely as polite people do, feeling awkward, wanting the conversation through. I watched her with hesitant caution after that day, and my visits lessened to the Irish Café. But later I pondered what makes up a life that we so easily discount, reducing it to the mere sound of a name.

And after a final visit and meal I approached the old register. It had never changed nor had its operator. But eyes had darkened, a blank face had lost its smile.

Next month I'm closing for good.
Hope you come in to wish Ol' Belle well,
She said with a shaky voice.
There is no reason to continue on.
As it is
most people eat elsewhere now.

Though I never returned I remember that last conversation, a crystal-clear moment in memory from then till now. As I turned to leave, a light touch on my sleeve beckoned my attention back.

Do you know my son?

She asked as she pulled a pocket size photo from a tattered, cracked brown, leathered purse. Pete, I had known in school, but not all that well, an upper classman, and only who he was by sight. But I had read the papers. Knowing what was to come, I waited awkwardly, absent of present mindedness.

After the TET offensive he's listed as MIA you know.
He is my only child.

How we used to tease old Belle, kid her about her age, her lipstick and rouge, her bright purple dresses, her favorite Bing Crosby, Perry Como, Dean Martin, and Tony Bennett music that echoed daily through the café, seeking a laugh for our ego, knowing she would graciously go along. On our part, we never recognized her struggle buried within, or the pain that was to come.

I saw her for a last time one early evening walking home on Cherokee Street a few blocks from the café now with a different owner and name. She held a paper sack full of groceries, a black shawl over her back, a thick scarf covering her head, a tattered dress . . . a defeated body, a lone soul, disconnected, moving through a gray-darkened day against a cold wind. I thought then and there to offer a ride, but I drove on by due to silly youthful pride. Those last images of her circle through my mind now and then. She faded from existence without my even knowing when. A life full of stories and drama, known only by a few. She was just old *Belle* who no one really listened to. Another someone who walked through life, a little bit odd, not all that attractive as shallow standards go. Someone to acknowledge in passing, but not with whom to spend time. But someone like so many with passions and life's lessons she had to bear, concealing a torn heart, about which most people preferred her not to share.

When on occasion I think of *Isabelle Hardy*, I wish to the memories playing in my head, and historically revise how it might have been, and how I would have changed and become a different man in time

175

if only I had attended and listened to the heart she had to give. The many crossroads I confront come to mind, the many who cross my path seeking only to be acknowledged. If I had taken the time to stop and listen how might I have been different? What different roads might I have traveled?

Then I ponder the notion of what in fact it's like to walk through life – unknown.

Austin, January 2013

Accidental Voyeur

In a small dip of a canyon carved in the base of a mountain I watched her walk toward the sylvan lake that hid in the crest of surrounding mammoth rocks and thin towering pines. The water lay like an enormous piece of blue emerald beneath the burning sun. The hard canyon rock and broken pebble at the water's edge soaked up the midsummer heat of the day that she felt rising into the soles of her bare feet. In her unabashed nudity, she gingerly but sensually approached the edge of the shoreline. The muscle tone in her body spoke of her being a runner and how well she cared for herself. And then in smooth strides she glided into the water like a skill-crafted boat embarking on a voyage. She descended into the natural pool until it reached just below her shoulders. The warmth of the primal mountain lake appeared to sink into her soul, and her body let go of its tightness. She breathed deeply and suspired a long-felt release.

Austin, January 2015

Incongruous

The rotting, decomposed remains of a now partially petrified schooner lay in an archeological dig in the midst of an expanse of sand, prairie grass, and cacti with ants, lizards, and scorpions crawling through and around the blighted matter. As far as the human eye could scan, plateaus and foothills dappled the distance. The sails that had once rode the wind had long dissipated, and only small smatterings of two masts remained faintly limned in the sand. Covered in dust, eaten by decay, the vessel once proudly possessed a time and a purpose that no longer existed, that no longer spoke of the living. Its shell lay like carrion consumed by emptiness, silence . . . nothingness.

The discoverers scanned the horizon to place the artifact in a setting that made some conceptual sense but only beheld the vast dryness of desert and drought. They formulated questions that seduced their catholic minds, questions for which, they zealously contended, there could be no final resolution.

Austin, July 2013

7:02a.m.
(Cherokee Lake)

I'm awake while mom and dad still sleep in the lake cottage bedroom. I quietly tiptoe onto the screened porch, lift the latch on the screen-door, and step into the morning. The sunlight is soft, lambent upon the lake, illumining large parts of it, but leaving its edges near the shoreline in the morning shadows beneath the pin oaks and long-needled pines. As I walk toward the boathouse the silent morning is broken only by the sound of mallards or mud ducks, an occasional flop of a catfish or bass, or a nutria slithering through some cattails. The bottoms of my tennis shoes are soaked with dew, leaving wet footprints on the wooden-planked pier as I walk to its edge and scan the morning scene.

A thin morning water vapor, hovering at spots, emerges from the lake as the sun strikes it and stirs its sediments and awakens the teaming life within. The nocturnal hunters and feeders have scuttled below to the sandy bottom to sleep off the day until the sun retreats once again. Stumps of burnt trees from the past, scattered across the lake, protrude from beneath the waterline where at one time they were rooted in life, providing glimpses of work carried out by the Corp of Engineers. The man-made lake, appearing natural as any throughout East Texas, is calm, the sunrise fresh with odors. The smells of sandy water, muddy banks, fish, and turtles all rise with the sun that has driven off the night, forecasting the heat of a summer day.

But for now living is the morning.

Austin, May 2013

Trolling through a Memory

He punctured the red wiggler's body sliding it onto the point of the hook around the crown and over the stem. It continued to wiggle and writhe, completely camouflaging the fishhook. My dad smiled and said, *Now, that's the way to hook a worm for fishing.* He lifted up a fishing line attached to a yellow-cane pole for all to see. The worm danced on the hook like a nerve ending on fire. He and Charlie took on the teacher mode for my cousin and I, two young kids giddy about a day of fishing with the *men*. We sat between his grandfather and my dad in the middle of the dark green fishing boat being silently propelled by a trolling motor. It glided soundlessly across Cherokee Lake that on an early still Saturday morning lay like a piece of blue-green glass beneath the east Texas sunrise. Occasionally a dog's bark from a shoreline in the distance would echo across the lake; otherwise there was silence except for the sound of the boat gently cutting the water and dad's paddling to steer it in whatever direction he wanted as though he was eyeing a particular spot on the water. When the paddle broke the surface, the sound of the water being stirred would awaken the silent morning. A sprinkle from the paddle intermittently dropped on my shoulders and neck as dad sculled one side, then the other. The lake water rolling off the paddle felt refreshingly cool.

While my cane fishing pole arched over the side of the boat and the fishing line floated in the lake, I would listen to my dad and Charlie talk quietly as though they would scare off the fish if they spoke any louder. They would talk about white perch, catfish, and bream – red ear, goggle eye, and bluegill – about cooking and eating fish, occasionally looking up at the clear sky, commenting on how hot the sun would get that morning. Fishermen believe themselves the best weather forecasters. *Deep-frying is the only way to go* they would say. And bream, perch, and catfish *taste much better than bass anytime.* I would listen while I watched the red and white plastic bobber waiting to signal a nibble or a hit. I tightly gripped the old yellow bamboo-colored pole like I wanted to hold onto it and the morning and never let them go.

Austin, May 2013

Night Fisherman

I watched him from the screened porch that wrapped around the lake cottage. He moved slowly but determinedly in the thick night tumid air that covered Lake Cherokee, July at sundown. He had built a thick-wooden counter with an old sink he had fixed inside of it on one side of the boathouse. He attached an old metal light fixture with two florescent bulbs that hung down from where he had strung an electrical line. June bugs and mosquitoes swarmed in the light. How he navigated the lake in the dark I never understood. I just always felt the angst of waiting his return. From the porch I would hear the boat motor echo on the lake, disturbing the melancholy chirping of the bullfrogs and crickets that signaled night had fallen. He skillfully channeled through the boat paths to miss the stumps just below the surface of the water, cut the engine, and navigated with the use of a paddle into the dock of the boathouse. Before coming in, he took time to clean the fish on the thick-wooden counter. I would watch the light go off as he retired for the night. After a shower, he sat with mom and me on the porch in the July heat, reading the newspaper below slow-turning ceiling fans hanging with porch lights. He needed neither the TV glaring, the radio blasting, nor the sounds and busy-ness of town. He could stay on the lake in its silence and never grow weary. He would be up at dawn and after a cup of strong black coffee, he would be ready to go at it again.

Then I didn't understand. I was too used to television and movies, hanging out with friends at the skating rink, driving up and down Highway 80, eating hamburgers and drinking cherry cokes, mingling at the drive-in. He probably wondered, as I grew older why I ceased going out on the lake with him all that much. When I recall this man's figure and movements on the lake, his skills, craftiness, and knowledge of the wild, the water, and the fish, now I too wonder. . . why.

Austin, May 2013

Lessons from a Summer Gig

Old man, take a look at my life.
I'm a lot like you . . .
—Neal Young

The old man settled back against the trunk of the huge pin oak in its surrounding and cooling shade that provided needed relief where we took our water break from the east Texas August. Countenancing a distant stare he spoke to me, but not to me, but to some far away place, some other time:

I remember when I was young, how being connected to the earth, the ground, the sky, the wind, the sun – a connection that would bring on a moment where I would take a deep breath, air filling my chest and stomach, surging through my inner being. And exhaling I knew it was good to know life. A type of ecstasy, completeness, fullness, and a sense of accord with total existence streamed through my body. Adrenaline pumping, brain sizzling, mind soaring, hormones racing. . . . . .

Too many seasons have since turned for me to know that feeling again.

Austin, May 2013

Spin-Offs

We called them spin-offs. In northeast Texas we didn't get the hurricanes that would blow into the gulf. Instead we got those heavy punctuated major thunderstorms that broke off the hurricanes like shards of glass from a shattered window being thrown in all directions. The forecasts would warn us about the impending storms. We would know they were upon us when the winds from the south would suddenly rise as if someone had turned on a fan the size of the universe. The warm May temperature would quickly become refreshingly cool, enlivening our bodies. From our patio doors I would watch as the sun became absorbed by the blackness of the clouds, and mid-afternoon would turn to midnight before my eyes. Sliding open a glass door, I could smell the water in the sky that contained a freshness that invigorated my senses and electrified my neurons. I knew the deluge was coming. The long-needled pines bent in the strong winds like a woman's long worsted flowing hair, swaying this way and that in a rhythmic dance. Dust and oak leaves swirled in mid-air. Acorns popped the top of the house rolling down the pitch of the roof onto the patio and into the yard.

When the storm hit the water poured out of the heavens as though an ocean floating above us became so heavy it could no longer maintain its flight. Thunder and lightning waged the sounds and scenes of war on the earth. We listened to the heavy fall in the tenuous security of our house. Finally the rain would ease as though someone turned off a faucet. Though silent from within the walls of home the rain had not ceased to fall, but had regained normalcy as if the storm offered a comment for what it rendered, saying: *For now I have vented to my satisfaction. For the moment all is okay with the land.*

Austin, May 2013

Maxine

When I was about nine-or-ten-years-old, one summer while out of school, mom and I drove to Lake Cherokee in East Texas to look at a lake home that was for sale. As we approached the driveway, the freshly white-painted mansion-styled structure immediately took on a homey feeling where it set stately in a grove of oak and pine trees beneath a hot Texas sun. We came face-to-face with a large screened-front porch matched by an identical balcony screened porch directly above it. The sound of water lapping on the shore on the lakefront side of the house broke the silence of the calm morning as we stepped out of the car. The present owner had left a key under the front-door mat for any prospective buyer. The screened porch was unlocked. As soon as mom turn the key in the front door and entered the huge two-story home, with a nuclear amount of energy she came bouncing onto the front screened-in porch ready to welcome visitors. She was an English bulldog, happy to see and meet anyone who entered her world. I jokingly ran from her hiding behind a chair. She immediately and playfully took to the chase joining me in a friendly game of frolic nonsense. Mom began to explore the house from room-to-room while Maxine and I galloped about, getting to know one another. For the nearly ninety-minutes that mom scanned the place, I also journeyed in-and-around, up-and- down the staircase and onto the lake-front balcony that overlooked placid Lake Cherokee, with Maxine of course, following closely behind me every step of the way. She had decided we were best friends, and devoted herself to never leaving my side. The owner of the house had left instructions that she was not to be let outside. So when I walked down to the lake's edge, she would look through a large picture window that faced the lakeside, impatiently waiting for me to come back inside and play. When I reentered the house, she would leap up-and-down with a silly bulldog grin on her face as though she had eternally been waiting my return. For about the last twenty-minutes of mom's surveillance, Maxine and I relaxed on a recliner on the large screened-in front, second-floor porch shaded by large oak trees in a breeze that cooled off the summer. Mom, too, came up to the upper front balcony, sat for a while with Maxine moving between us to determine who petted better. I knew I would not want to leave her when our time there was done. But mom and I did drive away, and Maxine watched us from a living-room window with a melancholy look in her eyes. Although mom loved the place, we never purchased the lake home. I never got to play with Maxine again.

Austin, September 2015

SOMETHING ABOUT MIDNIGHT:

An Afternoon Nap

I had a dream while napping one sunny spring Saturday afternoon . . .

Aunts and cousins were there reminding me of family visits from times past when I was young and we traveled for fun. I lay half asleep as my aunt and her daughter talked while the TV loudly broadcasted an Army-Navy football game. I thought how strange since it is May. (But my dad being a Navy man I was bothered that the Midshipmen were losing.) My mom walked in and began talking with her sister, impervious to TV football as she had always been. I thought it was good to have her back again. She mentioned she must take me to be fitted for glasses. It would take an hour out of her day. (I've never worn glasses in my life. I hope the dream is not a portent.) I wearily rose from my partial sleep, my mom and aunt smiling at me, and I walked into the living room. Boxes crowded the floor. Sacks of clothes and bric-a-bracs for traveling were packed and strewn here and there. The place was now dark. Suddenly aunts, uncles, and cousins were gone. (It always feels uncanny to me how in dreams, time and events fold and unfold as if our take on linearity doesn't quite grasp reality). I walked back to where I had been resting and my mom too was gone. I looked all around, feeling remiss that I had missed saying good-bye to everyone because I had napped the afternoon away. They had left and the place was empty except for me. I had the feeling it would be a long time before I saw any of them again. I was surrounded by the thickness of solitude.

I then actually awoke from my afternoon slumber and dream. The darkness was gone and the bright May sun angled through my

189

window-blinds. No football, no TV, no visit from family. I arose and walked to shake the nap from my head. I thought about mom and dad, all my aunts and uncles on both sides – they had all died some years back. And now once again I was in touch with how deeply I missed the times we spent together on vacations, holidays, and weekend get-togethers. And the bright spring day transformed a narrow inner cavern of sadness into a sobering sense of melancholic acceptance of how dreams canalize us through time.

Austin, May 2013

The *gods* on Mount Bonnel

This year the cool spring has hung on longer than usual in the Hill Country. We are not used to having to keep the heat on in late April and early May in Central Texas. On this now supposedly spring day as I stare out my bay window, the blue-grey wet skies and cool dampness remind me more of November than May.

It's funny to hear people complain. *When's summer gonna get here? Can't believe I'm wearing this sweater tonight.* Of course it's still snowing from Minnesota to Colorado, but here we think it's *cold*. Come mid to late August or early September when the heat has born down upon us for the ninetieth consecutive day at a hundred degrees plus, people will be bellyaching. *When's fall gonna get here? Man, I sure miss those cool days back in May.*

Maybe it's because in truth *Mount* Bonnel is only a cliff overlooking the Colorado River. But if there are any weather gods up there, their whimsical weathervanes betray their Aeolian vagaries.

Austin, May 2013

191

Think I'll Be a Tourist (For Just a Little While)

We studied astronomy and geography. We looked at the universe and distant galaxies, and read about all the places where the sun shines on other lands as it does ours. I saw it. I was there. I stayed in Rome eleven days where it was seven hours later than back home. Touching down in Milan I saw the sun, felt the heat and then experienced the siesta with its cool reprieve in the Hotel Del Consoli. (I'm all for siestas.) When the Roman city awoke again in the early evening, I enjoyed an Italian opera, and came to understand why dinner is severed at ten in the evening and late night pleasantries are a part of Roman nights. I became vigilant of the Gypsy pickpockets but romanticized their lives in my mind. I was baptized in the waters of time via day tours in Rome and bus rides to Pompey, Naples, and Florence, and a boat ride to the Island of Capri. I was an eyewitness to history in the form of a man and a dog frozen in time by volcanic ash. I shopped the leather stores of Florence. I was awe-stricken by the Statue of David, the practice sketches of Michelangelo, and back at home base I was enthralled by paintings of the Sistine Chapel. I loved the fact that my hotel was in walking distance of the Chapel. And I stepped into the ancient wonder of the Coliseum with its floor checkered by archaeological digs, all standing in the history of republic and empire.

I walked the streets of Catania, Sicily, getting lost in the maze of avenues, stumbling into those seedy parts of the city, where probably I was lucky to get out alive. In a hotel in Catania, I celebrated Midnight Lights with the Swedes. I followed the steps of Goethe and Woody Allen on a day's train-ride to Taormina, overlooking the Mediterranean, basking in the beauty of its aesthetics, even as a tourist. I heard a variety of languages, none of which I could speak, but was glad they were spoken. And then there were the beautiful Italian women. There's always beautiful women. After seventeen days, I touched back down in Chi-Town, where I discovered I'm a tourist who was glad to get back home.

Austin, June 2013

South Lane Wells

At the speed of light, images flash upon the screen of memory. A 49 Ford, mom washing dishes looking out a kitchen window facing east, morning sunlight, a warm orange glow, angling across a pine-colored hardwood floor, a red and green swing set bought at Western Auto, a white doghouse with maroon shingles that dad built himself, the sound of trains on those tracks that ran east and west, an occasional hobo, sunlight beating down on oiled and tarred packed dirt roads, flames burning off natural gas, and a small, shingled house with a covered cement front porch. We sold that house for fifty-two hundred dollars in 1960. I could stand on either end of the crossbars of that swing set and see down to the railroad crossing all the way to Harrison Road, which converged with Jones Street that was named after our family. I was told a whole slew of Joneses lived there over the years and that I was related to them all. I've seen their graves in Fisher Cemetery, dating to the first decade of nineteenth century. All the images unfold in a stream of recollections. The Jones families, countless oil derricks on the East Texas countryside, the hardware store owned by my great uncle, the Methodist Church on the corner of our street facing Highway 80, and the East Texas farm-to-market roads we drove as avid fans of the high school football games. My dad would always drive. After a game, we always stopped at a good place to eat, scouting where the truckers packed the parking lots. They knew where the good food was located. They rarely failed us. And then there were our family rituals, the kind one never wants to let go of. Catching the late night TV movies. Dad was a film projectionist during his younger days. He had seen them all, but he wouldn't spoil the plot for us. We owned a tall jukebox-like radio, on which we listened to the pops of the day. Gogi Grant (*The Wayward Wind*), Tennessee Ernie Ford (*The River of No Return*), Hank Williams, and everything he ever recorded. We relished in our summer fish fries, real Christmas trees that dad and I cut down, and bowl games on New Years Day.

Summers away from school . . . My school was all on one campus, first through twelfth grades, some of the same teachers my dad had. Make the grades, go to college, don't be a failure, fear's a hell of a motivator. Summer jobs, Louis Morgan Drugs (store # 2 that is), delivering auto parts, driving Highway 80, which ran all the way from the East to the West Coast. As a kid I used to think: *Wow, that's a long highway.* That was before Interstate 20, on which I headed west to my first job away from home. And then came the decades away from home. The passing of time begs memories to emerge like images on a movie screen. Sitting in the swing set, bathed by the east Texas sun, seeing mom look east at S. Lane Wells out the kitchen window that set above the sink. I could hear her sing, and can still hear her now signing, *Across the Wide Missouri*, while she washed dishes . . .

Austin, June 2013

Sunday Dinner at Mama Josie's

Musty smells from an old house built in the 1920's, red-metaled chairs, a shaded front wooden porch with blue-grey paint peeled by weather and time, dusty carpet and drapes, mothballed closets, framed pictures of relatives during WW II (one of my uncle who was wounded in the war). Green linoleum dinning room floor, yellow-faded kitchen floor, a blue carpet with yellow roses covering the living room. Sunday metamorphosis: smells of cooked corn, cornbread, purple hull peas, collard-greens, fried chicken and fish, mash potatoes, a bowl of gravy with steaming smoke swirling around the table, all prepared in timely fashion by grandma. Glasses jingling with ice, waiting to receive tea, grandpa enthroned on his corner chair. Grandma crying at the big dinner table, the day after his heart attack. Uncles, aunts, cousins, saying grace in King James English, laughter, jocosity, adults discussing grown-up things while cousins debated the talents of Ted Williams and Mickey Mantle. Dessert afterwards: banana pudding, chocolate pie, watermelon in the backyard, or homemade ice cream. We all waited turns to crank the handle. Afternoon sounds from the radio from which Dizzy Dean called the Cardinal's game, touting the prowess of Stan Musial. Grandpa lying back on stacked pillows with his shoes off listening to them *play ball*, easing the pain of the corns on his feet. Silence falling over the house as family left in two's, three's and more, hot sun descending below the horizon, the ride home with the melancholic thought of the eternity of days that fill one's life, having to wait for another Sunday.

Austin, June 2013

Morning Memory

Maybe I was five, perhaps six, that specificity I do not recall. But what I do remember is one early morning as I walked from the kitchen to our living room after breakfast, I encountered an inexplicable experience of time, place, and presence that spawned an emotional and spiritual fulfillment that I have never shared with anyone. Our small, wood-framed house faced east. The sunrise angled through a screen door decorated with wrought-iron patterns in the shape of flowers and leaves. The shadows of the screen door and its ornate décor lay framed on hardwood pine floors in a pool of red-orange glow from the morning sun. I stopped in front of the door, took in the peaceful, calming scene of warmth, light, and color, and I said to myself:

I want to remember this time standing right here for the rest of my life.

Austin, January 2015

Things that Sink in Deep

When I was growing up my family and I loved dogs. We owned several across the years. We always cried when they died. One was a brown boxer that for whatever reason we neglected over the years. We let him roam the neighborhood, get into dogfights with neighbors' pets, become the terror of the streets around our block. One evening, along with some other dogs where we lived, he was poisoned. He didn't die. But afterwards he walked with a severe limp. He changed over night from an attractive boxer to an ugly site of a mongrel. His appearance, movements, and vicious attacks on other dogs led people to fear and loathe him. Yet with people he was gentle and kind. He began venturing to the school I attended. Because of his grotesque appearance I didn't want to admit that he was my dog. One morning I watched him through the windows of one of the classrooms where I waited for the first morning bell to ring. His limp, scars from fighting, and slobber hanging from his mouth frightened people. A student approaching him froze when she saw him. A girl sitting behind me exclaimed, *That's the grossest dog I've ever seen.* But I had known him from a puppy; she hadn't. I had massaged his sore muscles after he had been poisoned; she hadn't. I had known what he was before he became what he was; she hadn't. Nonetheless her words penetrated deeply, generating a knife-like pain. That scene and those words have stuck with me to this day. I wish I understood why that one moment is still so crystal clear to me even now.

Austin, October 2015

198

Something About Midnight

There's something about midnight.

As I sit here staring out the window into the star-filled night, I know – I feel – I believe there is something special about midnight. It's not all good; it's not all bad. It's not all dark; there is some light. But it's not all light. I fall upon the silent quiet I hear and find my solace. Depending on the season I might listen to distant voices in the street, or I might hear a bitter wind chilling the city with a thin layer of ice. It's rather banal to say that it is a time that I can think and work without interruption. Sometimes banality is reality.

Dawn rises, night falls, midnight hovers. I like how it hovers. No interruptions, no emails, no phone calls, no scheduled meetings, no lunch breaks. Just the deepest time of night when I can rest in solitude where time, space, the hour, all belong to me. No one around to break the focus, no other voices forcing themselves into my mind, no coffee time, no beautiful women providing distractions. The hovering canopy of the end of night speaks to the need to bathe in anonymity – the silence and I. As I sit here staring out the window, I know – I feel – I believe.

There's something about midnight.

Austin, May 2013

199

The Forgotten Man

He appeared to take note of all that surrounded him but he said very little. He would nod to show his approval, lightly snort to sound his disapproval, but he didn't seek to persuade where he thought the time might not be worth the effort or the energy expended. He would show soft eyes where he agreed, but a stern look when he disagreed, but rarely entered argument for the sake of argument; instead he preferred to let those who so chose to go their way and bear their consequence. He worked from early morning hours until early evening hours, and rarely late into the night when work required. Although he was college educated, and people surmised he was well read, he bore the epithet *clerk* all his working life, which took place in the same office for the same company. He took a thirty-minute lunch, which he brought to the office in a brown bag, placing it in the refrigerator before setting at his work desk. Once every two or three months or so, he would take a lunch hour on a Friday, meeting his wife at a restaurant on the square of the small town in which he lived. Contrarily to the milieu in which he was ensconced he never sunk deep into debt, but saved for any huge and costly expenses he believed to be necessary. He maintained this routine through a rigid ethic for over fifty years, bearing his responsibility to his family, to whom he hoped to leave a little something that would give them the edge they needed to move on with their lives. On his shoulders he believed they could rest for their security and wellbeing. To abdicate such a responsibility was for him the acme of immorality. Because he didn't like politics or politicians, he never entered political debates, or never uttered a word regarding for whom he voted, or if he even voted at all. He had experienced a World War but never wanted to discuss what he had seen and done. As time wore on, many viewed his clockwork routine for living as a rather comical anachronism. All the people who transacted business with him, however, never once doubted his honesty, integrity, and skill, but they wondered who knew him on a more intimate level. Did he have friends, or what did he do for entertainment? After all, there was a TV in the family living room, a tall box radio left to him as a family heirloom that still worked wonders, and a record player next to a stack of records, primarily Jazz and Classical music dappled with some pop singers of swing from the '40's and early '50's. No one knew whether or not to call him a successful man. To say he was a quiet man would be an understatement. But when he died, his family wept and grieved deeply. A few others attended his funeral. For some time after his death people would comment about how dependable, trustworthy, and honestly he had lived his life. They admitted that they knew little else about him.

Austin, May 2017

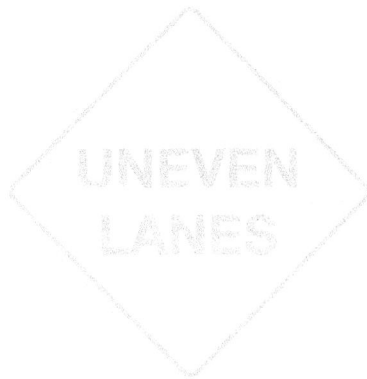

PLAYING WITH HAIKU

Haiku Poems

The woman of night
covers darkness with laughter
her joy a lie

The dawning morning
fades into the noon of day
waiting for the night

The end of searching
signifies a finished life –
cease not with movement

I sought transcendence
fell into eternity
back to space and time

Autumn paints summer
winter rushes in unmoved
spring thaws the hard freeze

At the dawn of day
awake and find your meaning
before nightfall comes

Consciousness of time
negates darkened timelessness
by choosing and not

Time is constant change
we live past-present-future
flowing seamlessly

Desperate with hope
the presence of your absence –
dreams of your return

Seeking to know none
we abolish the other
become the unknown

Watch rivers break free
rising floods face no limits –
resist containment

Yellow wildflowers
the predator feasts on prey –
ecstasy and pain

Kidnapped by the past
held hostage by tomorrow
we lose our today

In the loner's place
there is no need for the crowd –
golden solitude

The storm hides the pass
stay to die, risk forward on –
oh what a brave death

The East Texas sun
oil and tarred dirt black roadways –
memories surface

Lake Cherokee lies
wrapped in an East Texas dusk –
calm beckons the soul

Body grounds us deep
mind soul and heart seek meaning
spirit transcends all

Hear the werewolf call
incarnadined killer moon
blood lusts served in full

The wolf howls by night
runs by the stark light of day
returns to full moon

The Steppen' Wolf lives
alone away from the pack
solitary bliss

Midnight hides morning
in a blanket of darkness
dawn calls those who seek

Storms hinder the way
face the wind or quail in fear –
travel what you carve

The night the storms came
thunder and lightning waged war
daybreak crisp and clear

Come the storm of life
chaos challenges the wise
calm at the center

Evil will rob you
surrender all externals
treasure what is deep

Behold any man
who is calm while he suffers
fear but revere him

Lone highway unfolds
reflection of life's journey
in fear and trembling

Do you hear the call
that belongs only to you
then follow – follow

The path of the wind
look back to its origin
lose its destiny

The highways unfold
beyond distant horizons
seek not to stand still

East the sun rises
west it falls beneath the dark
cycles of life turn

Black and white image
lone figure beneath streetlights
a winter night snow

Dad beneath the sun
skillfully fileting fish
laughter and joy

Oracles declare
that place in which to find *there*:
its name is *nowhere*

Wildfire has its run
scorched black earth and all is done
green breaks to the sun

Deep in distant woods
echoes of lost lonely cries –
cowbirds' awkward call

Galveston shoreline –
small seashells pressed in the sand
glisten in the sun

Hidden in shadows
behind glows of neon lights
darkness softly calls

The humming bird rests –
a leaf clinging to its bough
camouflaged in green

Highway Eight-Four –
on the wind beneath the sun
the cry of a hawk

Before your presence
I will find calm in the light –
even in the dark

Into deepening
I wait upon the Spirit –
He will take me there

Submit all your ways
upon the altar of God –
He will set your paths

On a foundation
of embittered principles
a house cannot stand

Started: 11/24/12
Finished: 05/31/17

UNEVEN
LANES

AFTERTHOUGHT

Afterthought

Mr. Serendipity
had an epiphany
that the timing was wrong.

Lovely Casually
had a casualty
and the time was gone.

I'm into rocket science
and I make my alliance
with whomever I please.

I create that crazy fuel
sell to any raging fool
so they call me a sleaze.

If you want to be existential
pay attention to your potential
otherwise you're inauthentic.

If you lose your authenticity
your search for felicity
will lead you into a clinic.

Austin, May 2017

www.ingramcontent.com/pod-product-compliance
Lightning Source LLC
Chambersburg PA
CBHW071525040426
42452CB00008B/899